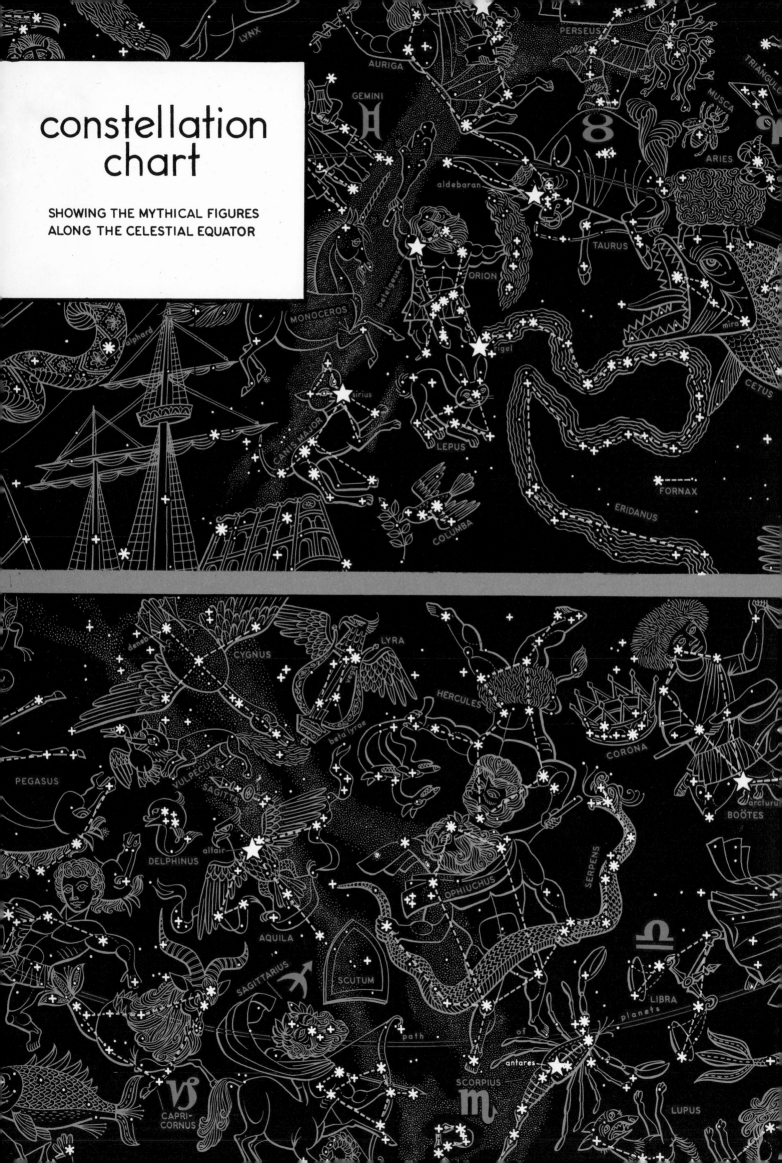

constellation chart

SHOWING THE MYTHICAL FIGURES ALONG THE CELESTIAL EQUATOR

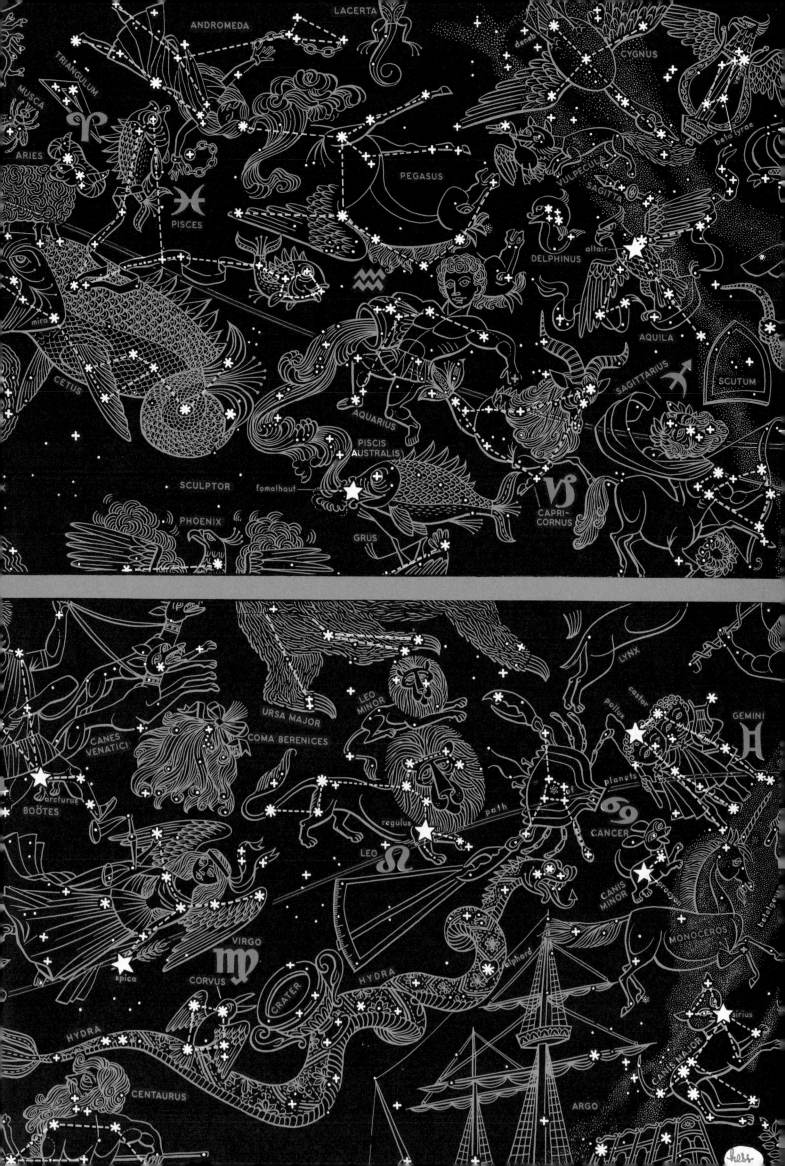

Exploring the Universe

REVISED EDITION

BY ROY A. GALLANT

ILLUSTRATIONS BY LOWELL HESS

Doubleday & Company, Inc., Garden City, New York

FOR JONATHAN AND JAMES

Roy A. Gallant has written many books and over 500 magazine articles, mostly on scientific subjects. In 1956 his book EXPLORING THE UNIVERSE won the Thomas Alva Edison Foundation Award for the best young people's science book of the year. He has worked on the staffs of *Science Illustrated*, *Boy's Life*, and *Scholastic Teacher*. Presently he is serving as consultant and author for a number of science education publishers and programs, including the Elementary School Science Project, in astronomy, of the University of Illinois, and *Nature and Science*, The American Museum of Natural History.

Lowell Hess comes from Oklahoma and is the oldest in a family of nine children. He is a free-lance illustrator and a member of the Society of Illustrators. His work has been published in most of the major magazines. He now lives in Southport, Connecticut, with his wife, two beagles and two cats. His main interests outside his work are Early American antiques, sports cars, woodwork, and Colonial houses.

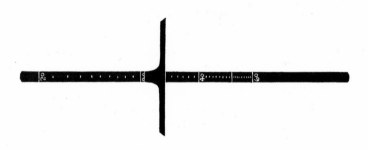

OTHER BOOKS BY ROY A. GALLANT

Exploring the Moon	Exploring the Sun	Man's Reach into Space
Exploring Mars	Antarctica	The ABC's of Astronomy
Exploring the Weather	Exploring Under the Earth	The ABC's of Chemistry
Exploring the Planets	Exploring Chemistry	Discovering Rocks and Minerals

The Author's thanks to Lloyd Motz, Professor of Astronomy, Columbia University, and to Kenneth L. Franklin, Astronomer, The American Museum–Hayden Planetarium, for their many helpful suggestions.

Contents

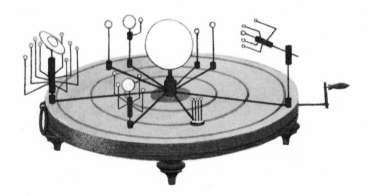

The Astronomer-Magicians

"Will the Sun rise tomorrow?" the student asked the astronomer.

"No," came the answer. "I say that the Sun will not rise tomorrow. Can you prove that it will?"

"Well," said the student, "my star book says that tomorrow, December 28, the Sun will rise at 7:12 A.M. Isn't that proof enough?"

"No," answered the astronomer. "That isn't *proof*. Your star book tells me only that some writer thinks that the Sun will rise tomorrow. Give me *proof*."

After a while the student gave up. He had to admit that he could think of no way to *prove* that the Sun would or would not rise the next day.

This little exchange tells us something very important about how astronomers and other scientists think and how they have tried to solve some of the mysteries of the universe we will be talking about in this book. They begin by asking themselves a question. Then they devise a test to find an answer. Nearly every day in your own home you devise tests or perform experiments, too, but you are usually not aware that you are acting like a scientist. For example, if it's a cloudy day, before going to work your father might ask you, "Is it raining out?" Chances are you will go to the window or stick your head outside to find out. On the other hand, you might tell him, "Well, I think it must be raining. Last night the newspaper said 'Rain Tomorrow.'" In this case your father probably would become impatient and find out for himself by looking out the window. He wants to know if it is *actually* raining.

To depend on today's newspaper for tomorrow's weather puts you in the same boat with the student who looked at his star book to convince his teacher that the Sun would rise the next day. But the student was asked to prove something beyond his power. All the star books in the world couldn't help him. All they could do was strengthen his belief that

5

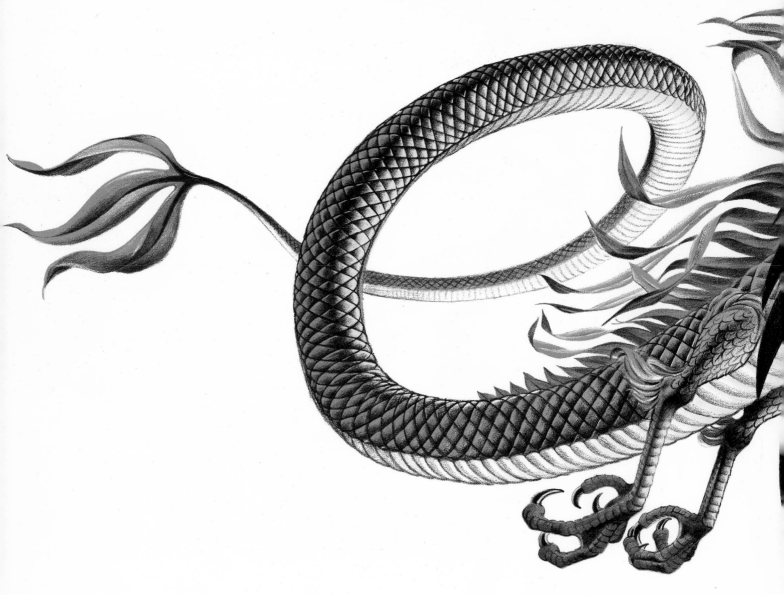

Dragon taking a bite out of the sun

the Sun would rise the next day because it has risen every day for as long as anyone can remember.

Luckily, not all of the problems of the universe are beyond proof. Today scientists have many special instruments that help them learn how far away the stars are, what they are made of, and why they behave the way they do. But in the days before cameras, telescopes, and spectroscopes were invented, men thought of the universe as a huge cosmic puzzle. And they saw so many pieces that they had little hope that the puzzle would ever be put together properly.

As far back as we can trace written records we find that men have been curious about the universe. Night after night as an endless sea of stars flowed across the heavens, men have wondered about those pin-

6

points of light and asked themselves many questions: What are the stars? Where do they come from? How large are they? Does our own planet shine like a star? What is the Sun's place in the universe? But early men had no way of finding the correct answers to these questions. Yet they tried. Nearly 5000 years ago in Egypt we find that men were very much interested in astronomy. But their interest in the stars was not to bring understanding to their fellow men. Nor was it to encourage the growth of knowledge. They were more interested in the political power that astronomy could bring them.

Why did politics and astronomy go so well together? Nearly 5000 years ago one of the world's great civilizations was centered in Egypt along the banks of the great river Nile. Farming was the main means of

7

livelihood for these people and the success of their crops depended on the Nile's flooding its banks every year. The annual flood was a signal for all agricultural activity to begin. But at this time in Egypt's history there was no reliable calendar to tell the farmers when to expect the flood so they could do their planting at the most advantageous time.

Egypt's King Menes, however, soon discovered a way to predict the coming of the flood. After years of observing the heavens, his court astronomers noticed that at the flood season the star Sirius was the last star to appear on the horizon before dawn. With this secret knowledge, each year Menes' court astronomers would announce the coming of the floods and advise the farmers to begin their planting. To the ignorant peasants, being able to predict the floods meant being able to cause them. So King Menes and his astronomers enjoyed the status of "magicians" who held the power to direct the course of all events. Or at least they made the people think that they held this power of magic. They knew that knowledge of the "secrets" of the heavens was a powerful tool.

Not all the astronomer-magicians of ancient times were as lucky as those who served under Menes. Some made blunders in their predictions and had to pay dearly for their mistakes.

There is the case of Hsi and Ho, two Chinese court astronomers who served under the emperor Chung K'ang, the fourth emperor of the Hsia Dynasty. Our story takes us back more than 4000 years, to a time when the Chinese believed that the Sun was forever in danger of being "eaten." Every so often, they said, dragons would sweep down out of space and attack the Sun, taking huge bites out of it. At such times the Sun would "go out" for a while, but its brightness would return after K'ang's men shot arrows into the sky, shouted, beat drums and heavy gongs. All this wild activity was supposed to frighten the dragons away, and so far as they were concerned, it did. The job of Hsi and Ho, the two court astronomers, was to predict when the dragons were going to attack the Sun so that K'ang's warriors could get ready for them. Today, of course, we know that the Sun's "going out" was nothing more than an eclipse.

8   The point of the story is that even 4000 years ago some astronomers knew enough about eclipses to predict them accurately. Hsi and Ho were two such astronomers. Their fame, however, did not last long because one day there was an eclipse that they failed to predict. Slowly the Sun

began to lose its light. It grew darker and darker until there was barely a glimmer. In great fright, Chung K'ang called out his men to fire their arrows, beat their gongs and drums to frighten away the dragons. To everyone's relief, a few moments later the Sun reappeared, so all was well —but not for Hsi and Ho. Emperor Chung K'ang arrested them and ordered that they be killed for neglecting their duties.

Astronomers think that this story provides us with the earliest record of an eclipse. But history is a bit fuzzy about exactly why Hsi and Ho were executed. A second version of the story says that the two unhappy astronomers misbehaved during the eclipse and were killed for that reason, not because they failed to predict the eclipse. Whatever the reason, we can conclude that being an astronomer-magician in those days was a dangerous business.

From what we have seen of the early astronomers so far, they made few attempts to study the heavens objectively. In other words, the astronomer-magicians were most interested in the personal power their secret knowledge could bring them. They never bothered to ask themselves *how* does an eclipse take place? Or *how* do the stars shine? Or *how* do they move?

Clouds of Fire

About 5000 years ago in India, there were astronomers who tried to solve the motion puzzle of the stars. These men were looking for a real explanation of the motion of the stars across the sky, and the Earth's place in the scheme of things. They imagined the Earth as a flat disk, and hanging above it was a huge dome. Attached to the dome and moving across it were the stars, Moon, and Sun.

Around 500 B.C. Greek scientists living during the "golden age of learning" also tried to explain the motions of the stars and tried to understand what made them shine. Like Indian astronomers before them, they were not interested in the personal power such knowledge would bring them.

One of the earliest of these men was Anaximenes, a teacher. He taught his pupils that the Earth was flat, "like a table" hanging in the air. All the stars and the planets, he said, were made from moisture rising from the ground. As the moisture rose, it became thin and changed to

9

fire. And so the stars were born. He also told his pupils that there were no stars under the Earth-table. The stars, he said, move around the Earth "as a cap turns round our head." And "the Sun is hidden from sight, not because it goes under the Earth, but because it is hidden by mountains, and because its distance from us becomes greater."

Xenophanes, another Greek philosopher, said that the Earth was a large rectangle floating in space. And the stars, he said, are clouds which each night are set on fire and rise into the heavens. The Sun, he told his pupils, gives us heat and light, but the Moon does nothing and is useless.

Heraclitus said that the stars were all made of fire, and that each one rested in a bowl. At night when we can see the stars, he said, the mouths of the bowls are turned toward us and we see their fire. But during the day the bowls turn upward and hide the stars from view.

Anaxagoras had one of the most imaginative theories of all to explain how the stars were formed. In the beginning, the Earth was a great spinning body, he said. As it spun around it threw off huge "earth stones" that became heated and that now shine in the sky as stars. When Anaxagoras announced his theory, he got into trouble for saying that the Moon and the Sun were nothing more than large stones. People of the day regarded the Sun and Moon as powerful gods.

For many centuries ideas like those held by Heraclitus, Anaxagoras, and others seemed sound enough. They seemed to account for the heat and light given off by the Sun, and for light coming from the other stars. When we read about Greek science in the light of the knowledge we have today, we should not be too hard on the old scientists. They were pretty good. It was the Greeks, remember, who first reasoned that the Earth moves around the Sun, although this idea did not gain wide acceptance until the 1600s. It was the Greeks, also, who first knew the shape of our planet and measured its size. They also calculated the distance to the Moon.

It is tempting for us today to think that we know all the answers; yet many of our ideas about planets, stars, and galaxies are wrong. But we will not know which ones are wrong until someone with more knowledge comes along. And that is really what science is all about: a lot of people trying to ask the right questions, finding and comparing answers, and then being able to give up old ideas when those ideas are shown to be wrong.

Dragons, Truths, and Trials

If we blame the ancient astronomer-magicians for their lack of sound thinking about the stars and planets, we cannot say that they lacked imagination. When they drew maps of the heavens, they passed on to us a most confusing picture of the stars, and one that has lingered on to this day—the constellations.

The Great Bear (part of which is better known as the Big Dipper), Draco the dragon, Cassiopeia, and many, many others, as shown on the front endpapers, are examples of constellations. As long ago as 4000 years, court astronomers in Babylonia were inventing constellations. Later, the Greeks and Romans added star groups of their own. In fact, as recently as the 1600s astronomers were still inventing constellations.

Nearly all of the star groups we use today were named many hundred years ago and come from Greek and Roman myths. They represent dragons, giants, serpents, and many other creatures. When we look at the stars on any clear night, we cannot tell how far away they are. Although we may see a bright star right beside a much dimmer star, we cannot say which one is nearer to us. The star that appears dim to our eyes may actually be a very bright star extremely far away; and the star that appears brighter may actually be a very dim star that happens to be quite close to us. The Sun, which is neither very bright nor very dim, seems terribly bright because it is only a few million miles away.

Apart from the Sun, all of the other stars seem to be the same distance from us. When we look at a constellation—Orion the Hunter, for example—Rigel, Betelgeuse, and Orion's other stars seem to be lightbulbs of different brightness all hanging from the same celestial ceiling. Although Betelgeuse seems to be the brighter star, actually it is not. Rigel is quite a bit brighter. It seems dimmer because it is nearly twice as far away from us as Betelgeuse is. If we could haul Rigel in to the

11

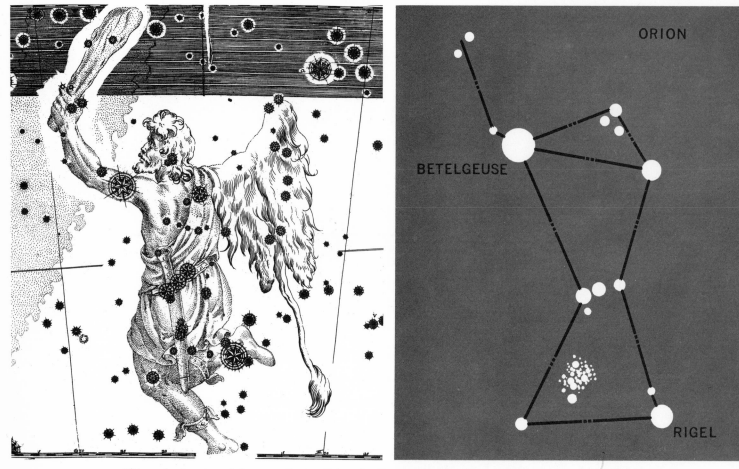

This early drawing of the constellation Orion the Hunter stretches the imagination. The relationship between Orion and the stars forming him leaves too much to the mind. It is much easier to find the constellation by imagining that the major stars are joined by straight lines.   The American Museum of Natural History

same distance as Betelgeuse, we would notice a striking difference in their brightness. And so it is with the other constellations. They are arranged in space like the leaves on a tree—some nearer and some farther away—not like raindrops on a window, which are all the same distance away. But the ancients could not know this. To their eyes, the stars were flaming torches hanging from the surface of a great celestial bowl that formed the sky.

12   Mapping the Heavens

Nearly 2000 years ago, Ptolemy of Alexandria gave the world an "official" map of the heavens. Although his map was not completely accurate, it was a step in the right direction. Ptolemy simply drew the constellations that had been handed down by the early Egyptians, Babylonians, Greeks, and Romans. Possibly he added one or two of his own. In all, Ptolemy's map showed forty-eight constellations. Today, astronomers recognize a total of eighty-eight star groups.

While Ptolemy's map of the heavens was an important gift to astronomy, his teachings about the Solar System were even more important. In the light of what we know today about the motion of the Sun and the planets, Ptolemy's ideas were wrong; yet in their day they were extremely important and were to set the stage for many important events for more than 1500 years.

First of all, Ptolemy knew that the Earth was not flat, as many of the ancients had believed. He knew our planet to be a great sphere. Up to this point Ptolemy's thinking was sound. But when he began to explain the motions of the Sun and planets, he imagined them to move very differently from the way we know they move today. Ptolemy's scheme placed the Earth at the center of the universe. The Moon, he said, circled the Earth. Next came Mercury, then Venus, the Sun, Mars, Jupiter, and Saturn. Each was supposed to revolve about the Earth in a perfect circle. In Ptolemy's system, the Sun was little more than an exceptionally bright "planet" circling the Earth as the fourth most distant object. Ptolemy also thought that the Earth was motionless—that it did not spin like a top. If the Earth did spin, Ptolemy reasoned, birds would have their perches whipped out from under them.

Today, of course, we know that Ptolemy's thinking was wrong, and we know that the planets do not move in circles, but in circle-like paths called *ellipses*. The reason Ptolemy chose circles is an interesting one. In those distant days the circle was considered to be the "perfect" form. Surely, Ptolemy thought, where the heavens are concerned there must be "perfection." So all celestial objects surely must move through the sky in circles.

Over the years Ptolemy's picture of the Solar System became the "official" explanation. The Church, which was extremely powerful during the Middle Ages, put its stamp of approval on Ptolemy's explanation of the Solar System. To believe in a different kind of Solar System was dangerous, just as it is dangerous in some countries today to hold certain political beliefs.

13

The Slow Awakening

Nearly 1500 years passed before anyone had the knowledge and courage to show that Ptolemy's thinking was wrong. The enlightened person to do this was Nicolaus Copernicus, a Polish scientist and an officer of the Church. Copernicus was a cautious man, firm in his beliefs, yet reluctant to express his beliefs if they did not agree with what the Church taught. About the time Columbus set sail for America, Copernicus began studying astronomy at the University of Cracow, in Poland. Next he went to Italy, where he continued his studies at the University of Padua. And in 1499 he began teaching at the University of Rome. During this time Copernicus had been reading the old theories of the Greeks as set down by Ptolemy. The more he read the more he was convinced that most of Ptolemy's thinking was wrong. In the year 1530, when Copernicus was fifty-seven years old, he completed what was then the most startling theory on astronomy ever written. Today his theory is regarded as one of the great contributions to science.

The Sun, not the Earth, said Copernicus, is the center of the Solar System. The Earth is nothing more than one of many planets circling the Sun. The Earth spins on its own axis and so accounts for day and night. Our seasons are caused by the Earth's revolving about the Sun. And the stars, Copernicus said, are great fiery globes so far away that we cannot begin to imagine their great distances.

When Copernicus explained his ideas to some of his close friends, they urged him to announce his theory to the world by publishing it as a book. Copernicus said no. He knew that the Church would object to his views, and that such a book would cause great trouble. Yet he believed

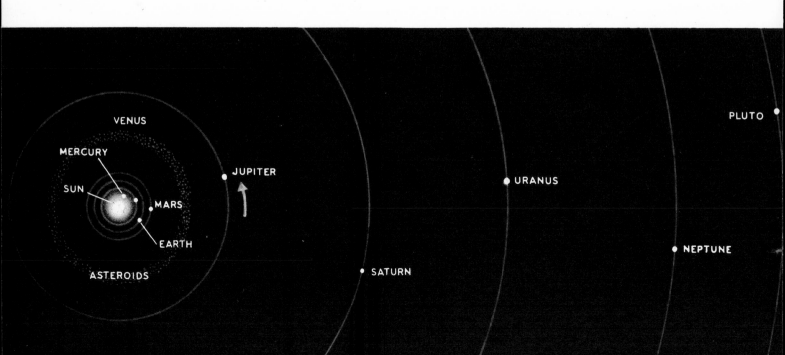

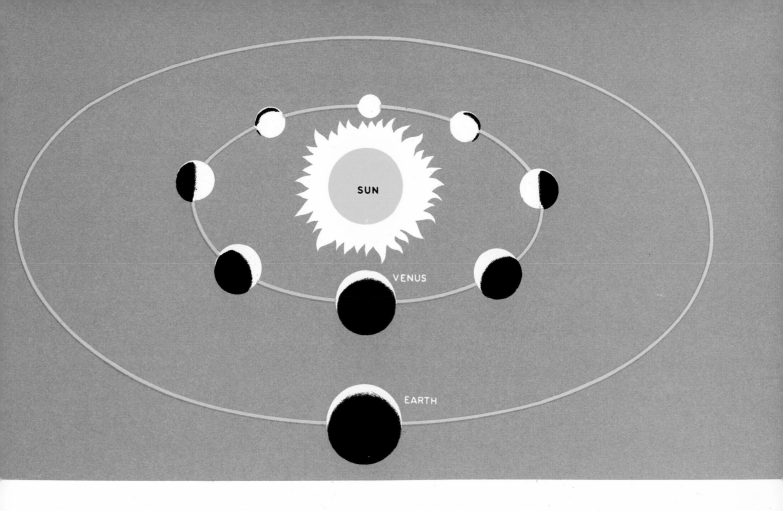

in his ideas about the Solar System. Finally, after thirteen years had passed, he agreed to publish his findings. The title of his book was *On the Revolutions of the Heavenly Spheres.* To protect Copernicus from an attack by the Church, one of his friends wrote the following words at the beginning of the book: "This is written to present NOT a scientific fact, but a playful fancy." As it turned out, there was little need to protect Copernicus. He died a few days after his great work was published.

One of Copernicus' admirers was an Italian scientist named Galileo Galilei, born in 1564. Galileo was convinced that Copernicus' idea about the Solar System was correct. But Galileo had no way to *prove* that what Copernicus said was true. He was in much the same position as the student who was asked to prove that the Sun will rise tomorrow.

In 1608, however, Hans Lippershey, a Dutch eyeglass maker quite by accident invented a telescope. Galileo heard about the discovery and within a year was hard at work studying the planets and stars through his new "optik tube." Imagine his thrill on first seeing the giant craters and jagged mountains on the Moon—and at peering into the depths of the Milky Way and realizing that this great shining cloud was actually

15

made up of billions of "suns." Night after night Galileo marveled at the wonders his telescope revealed to him.

As he watched the planets move across the sky, he noticed something strange about Venus. It behaved much like the Moon. At times it was "full," other times it was a crescent, and still other times it seemed to disappear. At once Galileo realized what this meant. Here was evidence that Copernicus was right—Venus was revolving about the Sun, not about the Earth.

Another discovery Galileo made was that the giant planet Jupiter has moons circling it. When he first saw moons of Jupiter, Galileo realized that he was gazing on a miniature model of the Solar System. It was time, Galileo thought, for the world to be shown proof of Copernicus' beliefs— in spite of what the Church might do.

Galileo wrote down his observations and then published them in a book.

When the Pope saw the book, he instructed Church officials to deny that Jupiter had moons and that Venus went through phases. Galileo, the Church said, has bewitched his telescope; do not believe the nonsense this man preaches. Galileo refused to be silenced. He continued to say what he believed was the truth about the motion of the planets. Finally, the Church summoned Galileo to trial and publicly forced him to deny that the Earth circles the Sun. According to legend, when Galileo left the court he was heard to say: "In spite of what I have been forced to say here, the Earth *does* circle the Sun." Today Galileo stands as a bright beacon shining through the darkness of superstition and hypocrisy. His concern for truth and his careful examination of the heavens place him among the greatest scientists of all times.

How Far to the Stars?

Although Galileo knew that the stars must lie at distances so great that the mind cannot imagine them, he could not prove that they did. The nature and distances of the stars were first described accurately in a general way by the British physicist Sir Isaac Newton in 1666.

Copernicus, the mathematician Johannes Kepler, and Galileo had set the stage for Newton. With an accurate map of the Solar System,

Copernicus had been wrong in one important way. He had thought that the Sun occupied the center of the universe. Astronomers later discovered that the Sun was but one star among countless billions of others in the universe. This photograph shows the northern Milky Way with its myriad stars. The dark band running through it is gas and dust, which blocks our view of many more stars hidden behind.

Newton was able to explain *why* the planets follow elliptical paths about the Sun. His theory of gravitation enabled him to do so. Since the planets obey the laws of gravitation, Newton reasoned, so too must the stars. The planets are held captives of the Sun by the gravitational attraction of the Sun. If it were possible to "turn off" gravitation, as we turn off a flashlight, the planets would fly off into space. Newton reasoned that the stars must be at very great distances from the Solar System; if they were not, they would be pulled into the Sun, or they would be captured by it and made to circle the Sun as the planets do.

He also reasoned that the stars must be other suns like our own, and in some way—unknown to Newton—produce their own heat and light. Because they are so far away, Newton reasoned, they would be too dim for us to see if they simply reflected light as the Moon and other planets do.

Nearly 200 years were to pass before astronomers learned the actual distance to a star beyond the Sun. In 1838 the German astronomer Friedrich Bessel determined the distance to 61-Cygni, a star in the constellation Cygnus the Swan. It turned out to be more than half a million times farther away from us than the Sun is. 61-Cygni also turned out to be one of our closest stellar neighbors! When it became possible to measure the distances to stars, astronomy took a giant step forward, and men had to change their ideas about the universe in many ways.   17

Among the questions they could now ask: Do the stars move through space, or are they motionless? Does the universe of stars have a center, or does it continue on without end?

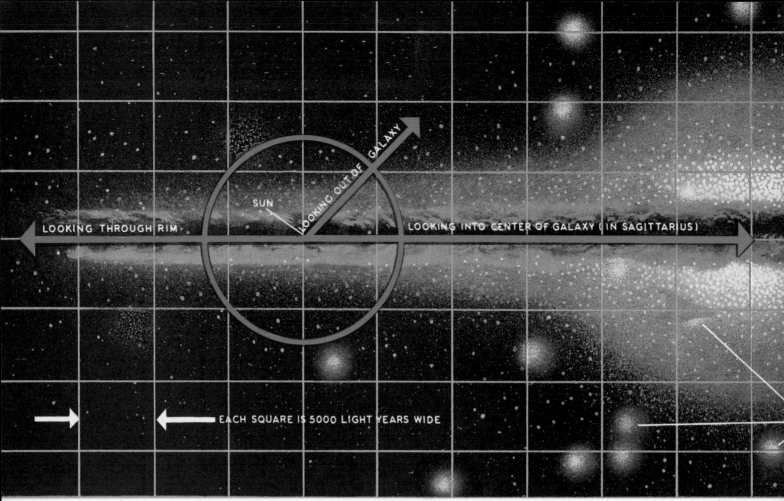

LOOKING THROUGH RIM

SUN

LOOKING OUT OF GALAXY

LOOKING INTO CENTER OF GALAXY (IN SAGITTARIUS)

EACH SQUARE IS 5000 LIGHT YEARS WIDE

Cross section of our galaxy

Exploring the Universe

On a clear night you can see about 3000 stars. A small telescope reveals more than two million. And through the 200-inch telescope at Mount Palomar, astronomers can see countless billions of stars. As bigger and better telescopes were built over the years, astronomers were able to peer farther and farther into the depths of space. As they did, they found an ever-increasing number of stars. The problem was to find out if the stars were arranged in an orderly way, as the Solar System is. Also, did the universe continue on and on forever, or did it stop somewhere?

After Bessel had found the distance to 61-Cygni, other astronomers began measuring the distances to other stars. But the measuring system Bessel used works only for stars that are fairly close neighbors of the Sun. To date, the distance to about 10,000 stars has been determined by the system Bessel used (called the *parallax* method).

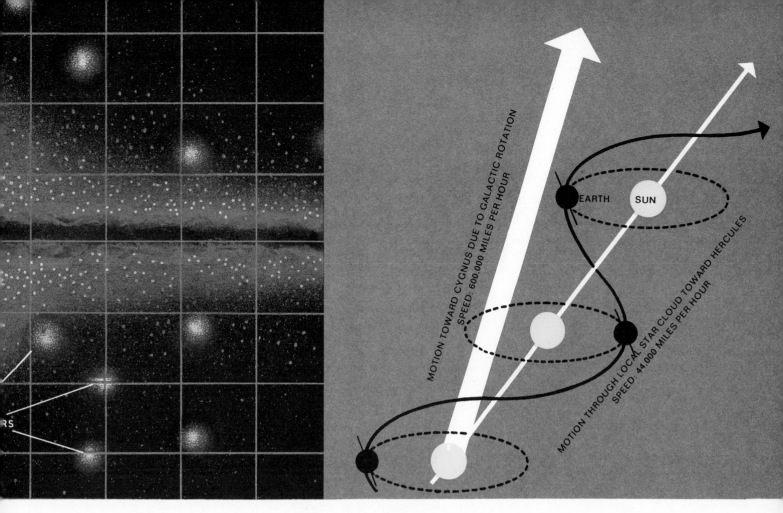

Motion of the Solar System

The distances to stars that are very far away from us were not learned until the spectroscope was invented. When attached to a telescope, this instrument separates a star's light into the individual colors of the rainbow, as a prism does. By analyzing a star's light through the spectroscope, astronomers can learn the *absolute* brightness of the star, or how bright the star actually is, no matter how dim it may appear to the eye. Then by using an instrument similar to a light meter, they can measure the star's *apparent* brightness (its brightness as seen by our eyes). When they compare the apparent brightness with the absolute brightness, they can then determine the star's distance. Until astronomers developed this way of measuring the distances of stars that are very far away from the Sun, they could not survey our stellar home, the galaxy to which our local star belongs.

19

Surveying Our Galactic Home

During any clear night when you look into the sky, you may see a luminous, hazy band of stars. Although you cannot see all of it at any one time, the band stretches all the way around the sky. The naked eye cannot resolve this vast star-cloud into individual points of light. Named by the Greeks, the Milky Way is part of the huge star system to which the Sun belongs. When Galileo and others first viewed the Milky Way through telescopes, they must have asked how the Sun and the other nearby stellar beacons fitted into the larger picture. But answers were not to come for 300 years.

The first surveyors of our galactic home were the British astronomer Sir William Herschel and his son, John (later, Sir John). In the late 1700s William Herschel tried to map the galaxy and show the Sun's place within it. He went about the task by pointing his eighteen-inch telescope in one direction in the sky, then counting all of the stars in that particular cone-shaped tube of space. Night after night he made star counts, selecting different parts of the sky one by one. One night, for example, his telescope might be pointed toward the Great Square of Pegasus and he would count all the stars visible to him in that cone of sky. And so he worked, systematically sweeping the sky of the Northern Hemisphere. When his telescope was pointed in the direction of the Milky Way, he counted many stars within a cone of space. But when it was pointed at right angles to the Milky Way he counted far fewer stars. What did it mean? Herschel wondered.

Sir John Herschel carried on his father's work, taking the telescope to South Africa in order to survey the sky of the Southern Hemisphere. When the work was finished, the Herschels had made nearly 6000 star counts. Then came the task of making sense out of the numbers. The Herschels concluded that we live in a great disc-shaped cloud of stars and that the Sun is located somewhere near the center. The Herschels, remember, made their star counts before Bessel and others had worked out a way of measuring the distances to the nearer stars. Without information about distances to the stars, the Herschels were not able to say, even approximately, how far it was from one edge of the galaxy to the other.

Matters remained pretty much that way for a century or so. The photograph on the opposite page shows a ball-like collection of stars

This globular cluster in the constellation of Hercules contains about 100,000 stars. A halo of about 100 globular clusters forms a sphere around the central part of our galaxy.   Mount Wilson and Palomar Observatories

called a *globular cluster*. We now know that 100 or so of these clusters, each containing about 100,000 stars, form a spherical halo around the central part of our galaxy. It was these clusters, and a special class of stars contained in some of the clusters, that gave the American astronomer Harlow Shapley the information he needed to correct and complete the Herschels' picture of the galaxy.

Shapley began his work in the early 1900s. He noticed that the globular clusters were not spread evenly all around the sky. Why? he asked. When he looked in the direction of the constellation Sagittarius, he noticed two things. First, that section of the Milky Way is the most

21

crowded with stars. Because it is, Shapley suspected that the center of the galaxy might be off in that direction. Second, he noticed that ninety per cent of the globular clusters also were off toward Sagittarius. Sometime after 1910 the idea occurred to him that the center of the galaxy might also be the center of the group of globular clusters. How could he find out?

The key was that special class of stars contained in some of the clusters, *RR Lyrae variable stars*. (We will have more to say about variable stars on page 44.) Like other variable stars, RR Lyrae stars pulsate in brightness. For a time they are bright, then they become dim, then bright again. As your pulse has a regular beat, so the RR Lyrae stars have a regular, but much slower, brightness "beat." All the RR Lyrae variables we know behave exactly the same way, no matter where we find them. Also, each one has the same absolute brightness. Shapley's task now was to measure their apparent brightness. Then by comparing the absolute brightness of an RR Lyrae star in any cluster with the same star's apparent brightness he could calculate the distance to the star—and so to the cluster.

This is just what Shapley did and he was able to say that the center of the system of globular clusters—and the center of the galaxy—were off in the direction of Sagittarius. Shapley's distance measurements told him that we are about 100,000 light-years from the center of the galaxy. The Sun, then, was nowhere near the center of the galaxy, where the Herschels had suspected it to be located. Although Shapley could not know it at the time, his distance was quite a bit off.

When astronomers talk about distances to the stars, they use a special system of numbers. If they tried to express stellar distances in miles they would end up with figures far too big to work with easily— 192,000,000,000,000,000, for example. To simplify matters they say that the star Sirius, for instance, is about nine *light-years* away. One light-year is the distance light travels in a year. Since light travels at about 186,000 miles a *second*, Sirius is 52 trillion miles away! Yet Sirius is considered to be a fairly close neighbor of ours.

22   To express a light-year in still another way, if the star Sirius should explode tonight, we would not see the flash of the explosion until nine years from tonight. It would take the light that long to make the journey to our planet. Because the stars are so very far away, when astronomers

see changes on those distant worlds they are looking back into time, seeing things that happened many thousands of years ago.

Shapley's distance to the center of the galaxy was off because astronomers at that time did not understand the effects of dust scattered throughout many parts of the galaxy. As you saw in the photograph on page 17, a long cloud of interstellar dust blocks our view of the middle region of the galactic disc. When Shapley measured the apparent brightness of the RR Lyrae variables in the globular clusters, he was looking through veils of interstellar dust and gas. The stars, of course, appeared dimmer when seen through the hazy dust than they would have appeared if there had been clear space all the way to each cluster. To Shapley, the globular clusters seemed to be farther away than they really are.

Taking the interstellar gas and dust into account, astronomers in recent times have been able to revise Shapley's distance figures. Applying our light-year yardstick to the galaxy, we come up with the following: The distance from one edge of the galaxy to the other is about 100,000 light-years. And the thickness at the center of our stellar disc is about 10,000 light-years. Located near the rim, our Sun with its system of planets is about 30,000 light-years from the center of the galaxy.

From our position near the rim we look edgewise through the galaxy toward the center, so we are unable to see it as a disc. It is like trying to figure out the shape of a cloud when you are flying through the cloud in an airplane. If we were able to look down on top of our galaxy, we would see something very much like the galaxy NGC 5457, on page 32. Astronomers estimate that the entire galaxy contains about 100 billion stars. Most of them are clustered near the center of the galaxy. In general, the farther out toward the edge of the disc we go, the fewer stars we find, and the greater the distances between them. Considering the vast number of stars making up the galaxy, only a few of them have been measured for distance, brightness, and so on. Measuring and naming every star in the galaxy would be an impossible task. For one thing, we cannot see them all. But even if we could, if we tried to name all 100 billion, it would take us more than 4000 years if we named one every second!

In recent years astronomers working with a major new tool—radio telescopes—have been able to tell us something about the inner architecture of our stellar home. Gas and dust in certain parts of the galaxy make optical telescopes as useless as a camera in the fog. But radio telescopes work very well in the "foggy" parts of the galaxy. With these newer telescopes, astronomers have been able to trace long curved lanes of gas. The lanes take the shape of spiral arms like those of the galaxy on page 32. Our planetary system, then, is a member of an "open spiral" galaxy and seems to be near the inner edge of one of the spiral arms. When you look at Orion, Auriga, Casseopeia, and Cygnus, all lying in the plane of the Milky Way, you are looking along our local spiral arm.

In the early days of astronomy, stargazers divided the heavenly bodies into two groups—the "fixed" stars and the "wanderers." The planets were called the wanderers because it was an easy matter to see them shift back and forth among the stars. But the stars presented a different picture. To detect their position change—different from their rising and setting motion—requires special instruments and many years of observation. They are so far away from us that they appear to stand still. For this reason the ancients called them "fixed" stars.

To "unfix" them took many years of observation. Today we know that the stars are moving through the heavens at many thousands of miles an hour. The old astronomers might have said, "If the stars move, then why don't the shapes of the constellations change?" Actually the constellations' shapes are changing, but so slowly that we do not notice the change. Many thousands of years from now the Big Dipper will have a completely different shape, as shown on page 26.

The Stars in Motion

About 250 years ago, the British astronomer Edmund Halley upset the "fixed star" idea of the ancients by saying that certain stars were moving through space. Halley had noticed that two stars—Arcturus and Sirius—were no longer in the position where the Greeks had put them on star charts 2000 years earlier. You need spend only a few minutes at a telescope to see that the planets are in motion. You can see them move against the background of stars, which seem motionless because the stars are so far away.

Detecting the motion of stars was very difficult until cameras were used in astronomy. We can take a photograph of the sky tonight then file it away. Dozens or hundreds of years from now other astronomers will be able to compare our photographs with their own and see how the positions of the stars have changed in a particular patch of sky. The motions of nearby stars appear swifter than the motions of distant stars, just as telephone poles and other nearby roadside objects seem to flash by your car while a hilltop way off in the distance seems to be moving hardly at all. Halley was able to say that Sirius and Arcturus were moving because they are so close to us (only 36 light-years for Arcturus, and 8.7 light-years for Sirius). It is much more difficult to detect the motions of distant stars. In general, it takes about 10,000 years for a star of a certain distance from us to move across the angular width of the Moon.

By studying the motions of thousands of stars, we now know that the Sun itself is moving among the nearby stars. It is headed toward the constellation Hercules. The picture we have of our local group of stars is a confusing one. We seem to be a wasp in a swarm, where each star-wasp is moving this way and that in relation to the others. But if we could move away from the swarm, or our local group of stars, we would see that the whole swarm is moving along; in other words, there is "order." As the planets all revolve around the hub of the Solar System (the Sun), the 100 billion stars of the galaxy move in orderly fashion around the galactic hub. The general picture, then, is that all of the stars in our local group are moving in an orderly procession around the center of the galaxy; but the individual stars forming the group move this way and that in relation to each other.

As the diagram on page 19 shows, our local group of stars, the Sun with it, is moving toward Cygnus, due to the rotation of the galaxy; but the Sun's individual motion through the local group is toward the constellation Hercules. Today, the stars Procyon and Sirius are near neighbors, but their motions relative to the Sun are such that 100 million years from now the three of us will be scattered far and wide.

The length of time it takes the Sun to complete one trip around the galaxy is called a *cosmic year*. About half a cosmic year ago, dinosaurs were roaming the land. Since the Earth was formed some five billion years ago, we have made about twenty trips around the galaxy.

The next time someone tells you that you are moving too slowly you can say that you are really traveling quite fast. If you are moving at two miles an hour you can add these speeds to your own: 1000 miles an

25

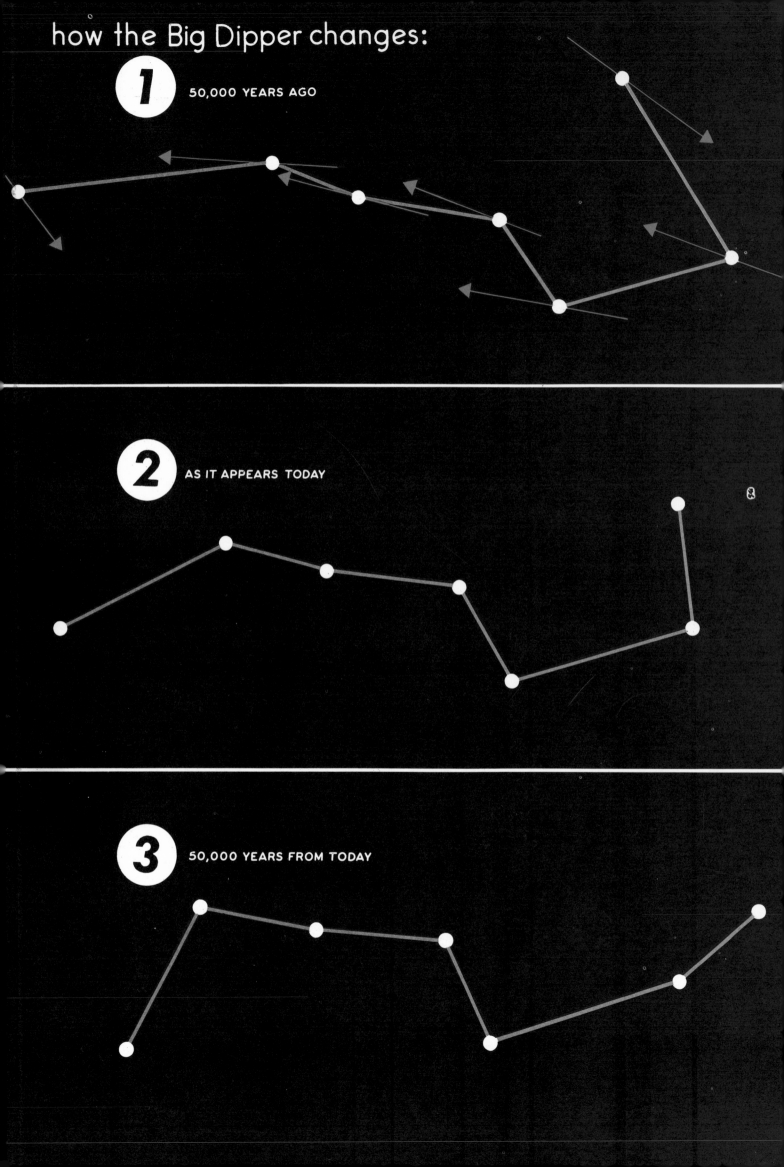

how the Big Dipper changes:

1 50,000 YEARS AGO

2 AS IT APPEARS TODAY

3 50,000 YEARS FROM TODAY

hour, which is the rotational speed of the Earth's surface at the Equator; 66,000 miles an hour, which is the Earth's speed as it circles the Sun; 44,000 miles an hour, which is the Sun's speed through our local group of stars; and 600,000 miles an hour, which is the group's speed around the galaxy. Your speed: 711,002 miles an hour!

The Universe Grows Larger

For many years, astronomers thought of the vast collection of stars seen in the Milky Way as being the entire universe. Beyond the limits of our star system there was nothing, only the black empty sea of outer space. If this were so, our problems of understanding the universe might seem much simpler than they are. For many years Galileo and his followers peered through their telescopes in an attempt to understand the millions of pinpoints of light shimmering before their eyes. Occasionally their view became blurred by huge clouds hovering in the dark regions of space. Usually they ignored these mysterious clouds and turned their telescopes toward a clear patch of stars and continued their gazing.

One such astronomer was a French observer named Messier. His main interest in astronomy was watching comets. While some people like to collect sea shells or military buttons, Messier liked to collect comets. For years he scanned the heavens, but too often he would find his telescope pointed at misty patches of light in the sky. He had little interest in them but he made a record of each one he saw, listing all of them as "objects to avoid." In 1771, he published a booklet containing a total of forty-five of the light patches, which we now call *nebulae*. Today the Messier list includes more than 100 "bothersome" objects.

Around 1773, when Herschel began his work in England, he suspected that Messier's misty clouds might actually be giant clusters of stars. For years he studied these clouds. Finally he drew two conclusions about them. One kind of nebula, he felt, most certainly was a series of giant star clusters. But the other kind, he said, was most likely made up of huge clouds of interstellar gas and dust. Both, he thought, were contained within the Milky Way. But as the years passed and Herschel studied the heavens more carefully, he began to wonder: Is there a possibility that these star clusters are not part of the Milky Way? Could

27

The "Great Nebula in Andromeda," the Andromeda Galaxy, as revealed by the 200-inch telescope. The two bright patches (upper right and lower left) are satellite galaxies. Mount Wilson and Palomar Observatories

they be many, many miles out in space? And if they are, does this mean that there is more than one "universe?"

It wasn't until 1924 that these questions were answered. The man to provide the answers was the American astronomer Edwin Hubble. Working with the 100-inch telescope at the Mount Wilson Observatory, Hubble found a way of measuring the distance to the Great Nebula in Andromeda.

Photographs of the Great Nebula in Andromeda showed many individual points of light that appeared to be stars, but Hubble could not be sure that they were stars. For all he knew, they might not even be part of the nebula. But he made the guess that they did belong to the nebula and that they were individual stars. It was a starting point.

As he studied the individual starlike objects, Hubble noticed that some of them changed from bright to dim to bright again, somewhat like the RR Lyrae stars that Shapley observed in the globular clusters. The pulsating stars that Hubble observed were also variable stars, but a super-bright kind called *Cepheid* variables. There are many such stars in our own galaxy. If the stars in the Andromeda nebula were, in fact, Cepheid variables, then Hubble could determine their distance, as Shapley had determined the distance to the RR Lyrae stars in the globular clusters.

Knowing the absolute brightness of the Cepheid variables from their periods, Hubble measured their apparent brightness. Then after making corrections for gas and dust between us and the nebula, he was able to say that the Great Nebula in Andromeda was about 1,000,000 to 750,000 light-years away. (In the early 1950s the distance was corrected to 2,000,000 light-years.) Clearly it was not part of our galaxy at all; it is about twenty of our galaxy's diameters away. Furthermore, the nebula revealed itself as a galaxy similar to our own but about twice as large. By studying the Andromeda Galaxy in detail, astronomers have been able to learn many things about our own galaxy. It is as though we were able to look at ourselves from two million light-years away.

With the discovery that the "nebula" in Andromeda was, in fact, a galaxy, the horizon of the universe broadened. We were no longer alone in space. And it continued to broaden with the discovery that more and more of Messier's "bothersome" objects were galaxies, not patches of dust and gas. The number of "island universes" in the heavens is stag-

The number of "island universes" in the heavens is staggering to the imagination. A good telescope brings into view more galaxies than the naked eye can count stars. The cluster of galaxies shown here is visible in the constellation Hercules.   Mount Wilson and Palomar Observatories

gering to the imagination. A good telescope brings into view more galaxies than the naked eye can see stars. If you examined only the bowl section of the Big Dipper, you would find at least half a million galaxies! In all, astronomers think that about a billion galaxies can be seen through our largest telescopes. How many more lie beyond is anyone's guess.

In our local region of space there are seventeen known galaxies making up what we call the *Local Group*. The two nearest ones, the Clouds of Magellan, are only 200,000 light-years away from us. Five others, which are dwarf elliptical galaxies, are also nearby companions. Any galaxy that is within about three million light-years of us is said to belong to the Local Group because we must look several million more light-years before coming to the next nearest galaxy, one which may belong to another localized group. Although only seventeen or so neighboring galaxies are known now, chances are that several others will be discovered.

1	spherical
2	elliptic
3	transitional
4	closed spiral
5	open spiral

NGC 4594 in Virgo, seen edge on.

NGC 5457 in Ursa Major

Mount Wilson and Palomar Observatories

One interesting thing about our Local Group is that twelve out of the seventeen galaxies are dwarf galaxies. And three out of the remaining five are spiral galaxies, like our own and Andromeda. If this small sample of seventeen galaxies tells us anything about the entire universe of galaxies, then large spiral types like our own are rare. But we must remember that only 17 galaxies out of the billion visible is a *very* small sample.

By studying and photographing many of the galaxies, astronomers have discovered several different types. There are the *spherical galaxies*, which are shaped like globes with fuzzy edges. Next are the *elliptic galaxies*, which are shaped something like eggs. The *transitional galaxies* look like large cosmic footballs. *Closed spiral galaxies* look like slow-moving pin wheels, while *open spiral galaxies* appear like a snapshot of a swiftly spinning pin wheel shooting out long arms of sparks.

32   The study of galaxies is so new that astronomers have not yet come to an agreement about what the shape of a galaxy might have to do with its age. Most astronomers suspect that there may be no connection at all. They think that all galaxies may be about the same age. Their dif-

NGC 4486 in Virgo

NGC 1300 in Edidanus

Mount Wilson and Palomar Observatories

ferent shapes come from the spinning speeds the galaxies were given at their birth and from the amount of dust and gas they have. Those having a lot of dust have spiral arms. The others do not.

The True Nebulae

If you should spend several nights at a telescope studying the Milky Way and its neighbor galaxies, you would probably become annoyed by several clouds that would spoil your view. These are the true nebulae—vast cosmic clouds of dust and gas. One of the most splendid nebulae in the heavens is one called the Horsehead, located in the constellation Orion. The matter forming the nebula is lighted by stars shining behind the cloud, and so the cloud takes on the shape we see. Astronomers think that these mammoth clouds are the stuff out of which the galaxies, stars, and planets are made. Another famous nebula, the Ring Nebula in the constellation Lyra, looks like a giant smoke ring floating in space. Actu-

33

The Horsehead Nebula, one of the most splendid nebulae visible to us, is located in the constellation Orion south of Zeta Orionis. Its catalog number is IC 434.　　　　Mount Wilson and Palomar Observatories

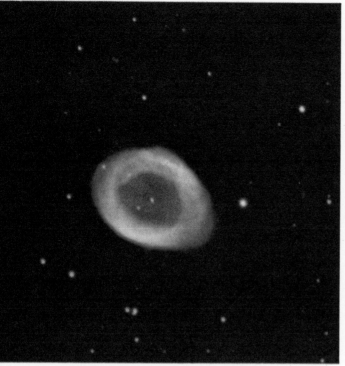

The Ring Nebula in Lyra, NGC 6720

The Crab Nebula in Taurus, NGC 1952

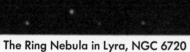

© California Institute of Technology and Carnegie Institution of Washington

ally it is a huge shell of gas continually being ejected by a star. Seen from a distance, the ring appears denser around its edge and so takes on the shape of a ring.

One of the most spectacular nebulae in the skies is one called the Crab Nebula. According to records left by Chinese astronomers, in the year 1054 a star was seen to explode. The result: a huge gas cloud that has been spreading out at the rate of 800 miles a second for nearly a thousand years. Today it stretches more than 42 light-years across.

The Birth and Death of Stars

To the naked eye the stars appear to be little more than flickering pinpoints of white light hanging in the black depths of endless space. Yet a close look, even with the naked eye, reveals them as jewels shining blue-white, yellow, and red.

Where do stars come from? How long do they go on shining? And why do they eventually go out? These are the questions today's astronomers are asking. Although the answers are not known for certain, we do have many clues that make us think that we may be on the right track in our search for answers. 35

The nebulae, such as the great dark "rift" we see in the summer Milky Way, especially in Cygnus, are probably the birthplaces of stars.

The Great Nebula in Orion, NGC 1976, contains enough gas and dust to make many stars the size of the Sun. Stars seem to be formed in such regions.   Mount Wilson and Palomar Observatories

The Great Nebula in the constellation Orion is known to have enough gas and dust to make many stars the size of the Sun. Among the several clues that make us think that stars form out of the nebulae are *globules*. Globules show up as dark spots on photographs of some nebulae. Measuring hundreds of millions of miles across, the globules are thought to be dense concentrations of gas and dust on the way to becoming a star. But how?

36

The globules themselves are formed out of the material of the nebula. Here and there in the nebula are patches of gas and dust denser than patches elsewhere. A larger patch attracts smaller patches, pulling the smaller patches into itself, and in the process the patch begins to spin. By collecting more and more gas and dust in this way, a particularly large patch becomes a globule.

While it is collecting itself, a globule heats up. The hydrogen gas and dust particles pack themselves tighter and tighter around the core of the globule. Under greater and greater pressure, the core material of the globule slowly begins to heat up. Eventually it becomes so hot that the dust particles are broken down into atoms and the globule begins to shine dimly. A *proto*star has been formed.

The material of the protostar continues to pack itself more and more tightly around the core and the temperature continues to rise. When the very dense core reaches several million degrees, hydrogen gas atoms (which make up about ninety per cent of the star) in the core smash into each other with such force that they fuse. This continuous fusion of hydrogen produces a gas called helium. As core hydrogen of the star changes into helium, great amounts of energy are released. Some of that energy reaches us as light. At this stage in its life, the star has begun to shine in the way it will continue to shine for the millions or billions of years of its "adult" life before entering old age. It is the way the Sun is shining now and the way nearly all of the other stars we see are shining. Hydrogen atoms in the stars' cores are smashing into each other and changing into helium. In the process, great amounts of energy are released.

Earlier, we said that some stars are blue-white, others yellowish, and still others red. How do they get this way? What color a star is to be during its adult life depends on how much matter forms the star during its infant globule stage. If the globule is particularly large and has a lot of gas and dust, the star becomes a very hot and very bright bluish-white adult star. The stars Rigel, Sirius, Vega, and Deneb are such stars. The adult life-span of these very bright stars is shorter than the adult life-span of cooler stars like the Sun.

If the globule is neither especially large nor especially small, it turns into a yellowish star like the Sun. Hydrogen-into-helium reactions in the Sun's core have kept our star shining for about five billion years. And there is enough hydrogen fuel left to keep it shining steadily for another five billion years. If the globule is rather small, the star that develops from it, such as Proxima Centauri, is reddish and is cooler than either the yellow or bluish stars. In general, we would expect that the reddish stars have the longest adult life-spans.

When you look at the stars on any clear night, their color can tell you something about their temperatures. The bright blue stars are the hottest, having surface temperatures up to hundreds of thousands of degrees; yellowish stars like the Sun have surface temperatures of about 6000°K; and the dimmer reddish stars, about 3000°K. But these are the surface temperatures, remember. Deep within the cores of all three types of stars, the atomic furnaces are raging at temperatures of many millions of degrees. (The "K" in 6000°K stands for degrees on the Kelvin temperature scale. Six thousand degrees Kelvin are equal to 6000 minus 273, or 5727 degrees on the centigrade scale, and to 10,800 degrees on the Fahrenheit scale. To convert from degrees K to degrees C, subtract 273 from the K reading. To convert from degrees C to degrees F, multiply the centigrade reading by nine, divide by five, and add thirty-two.)

Since all stars have only so much hydrogen fuel, they cannot go on shining forever. One day they must go out. A star enters old age when it has used up nearly all of the hydrogen in its core. When that day arrives in the life of a star, different reactions are touched off within the core. If the star is one like the Sun, it swells up from 50 to 100 times its normal size. At the same time, its surface cools. No longer is the star shining yellow, but reddish. At this stage it is a red giant. It takes a star like the Sun about 150 million years to reach the full red-giant stage, and it remains that way for many, many millions of years more.

Although we think we know what happens to a star after the red-giant stage, we are not at all sure *how* it happens. During 1862, Bessel observed that the blue giant Sirius traced a wobbly path through the heavens. The cause of the star's behavior was a small companion star. Together, the two stars circle each other and so account for Sirius' mysterious motion.

The companion star of Sirius shines with an intense white light. It is a star in its dying stages. It has used up all of its hydrogen and shines only because it is contracting—becoming smaller and smaller. Stars like this, in their last stage of life, are called *white dwarfs*. As they continue to shrink over periods of millions and millions of years, they become as small as planets. Gradually a white dwarf's light dims, eventually becoming so dim that the star is best described as a black dwarf.

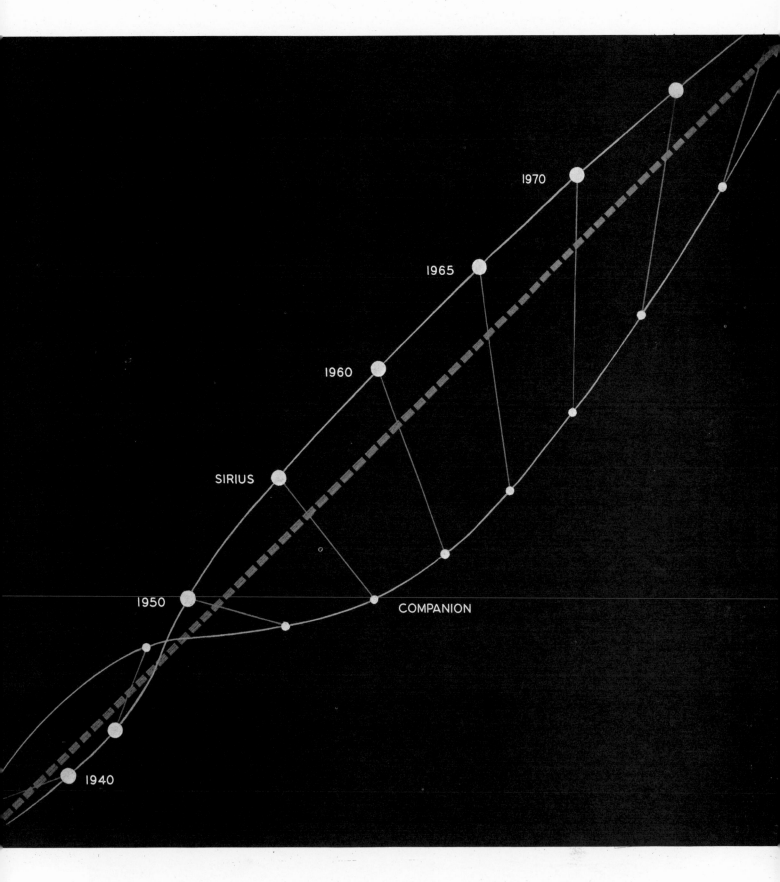

Sirius and its companion revolve about each other in much the same way as the ends of a whirling baton do as the baton is tossed into the air.

Stars That Explode

While most stars seem to die quietly and enter old age as white dwarfs, others cut their lives short by blowing themselves to bits. When we talked about nebulae on page 35, we mentioned a star in the constellation Taurus that Chinese astronomers saw explode in the year 1054. In the year 1572, Tycho Brahe saw a similar star in Cassiopeia. It was so bright that he could watch it during the day, but after more than a year it faded from view. In 1935, another extra-bright star, one in the constellation Hercules, went on a rampage, as the photographs on this page show.

Astronomers call these rambunctious stars *novae* (meaning "new") and *supernovae* (singular, *nova* and *supernova*). We know of about 150 of them in our galaxy, but have reason to believe that more than twenty new ones appear each year. Ordinarily, these are novae, not supernovae. Why novae suddenly become intensely hot and bright is still a mystery. When a nova is in the making, it suddenly begins to shine brighter and brighter until it stands out among the surrounding stars. It may remain bright for several months, then it may slowly dim and gradually return to its normal brightness.

Supernovae are much rarer events than the less active novae. When a supernova explodes, it may lose a good part of its mass, or it may utterly destroy itself. A supernova star may reach an absolute brightness 100 million times that of the Sun. We know of only three in our own galaxy— the Guest Star of 1054, Tycho's Nova, and Kepler's Nova of 1604. What causes novae and supernovae to go on a rampage is a puzzle. We simply do not know why they behave the way they do.

In 1935 the Nova Herculis showed a large decrease in brightness from March 10 (left) to May 6 (right).
Lick Observatory

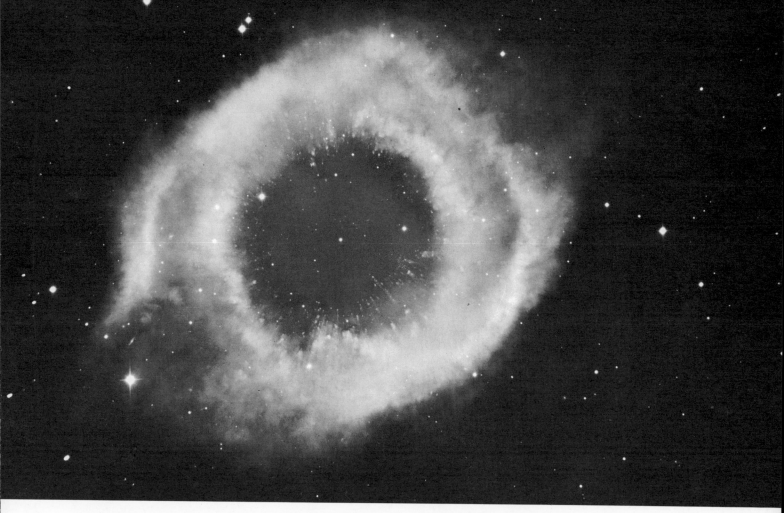

NGC 7293, the "planetary" nebula in Aquarius, is a great shell of gas expanding at a rapid rate.
Mount Wilson and Palomar Observatories

Just as puzzling are the erratic, high-temperature stars such as those forming the Ring Nebula in Lyra and the "planetary" nebula in the constellation Aquarius. As the photographs show, in both cases a central star is surrounded by a huge shell of gas resembling a ring. It appears as a ring because we see a greater thickness of gas around the edge of the shell than we do when we look into the shell toward its center. For reasons not yet known, these shell stars eject part of their gas out into space and the shells swell up at a typical rate of about 36,000 miles an hour.

An interesting thing about these stars, the novae, and the super-novae is that all of them are returning matter to space. In other words, they are providing material out of which new stars can be formed. However, from what we now know, only about one per cent of all of the material making up our galaxy is in the form of gas and dust today. All the rest is locked up in the stars and planets. This suggests that fewer stars are being formed today than several billion years ago.

We can imagine one time in the life of our galaxy when many stars

41

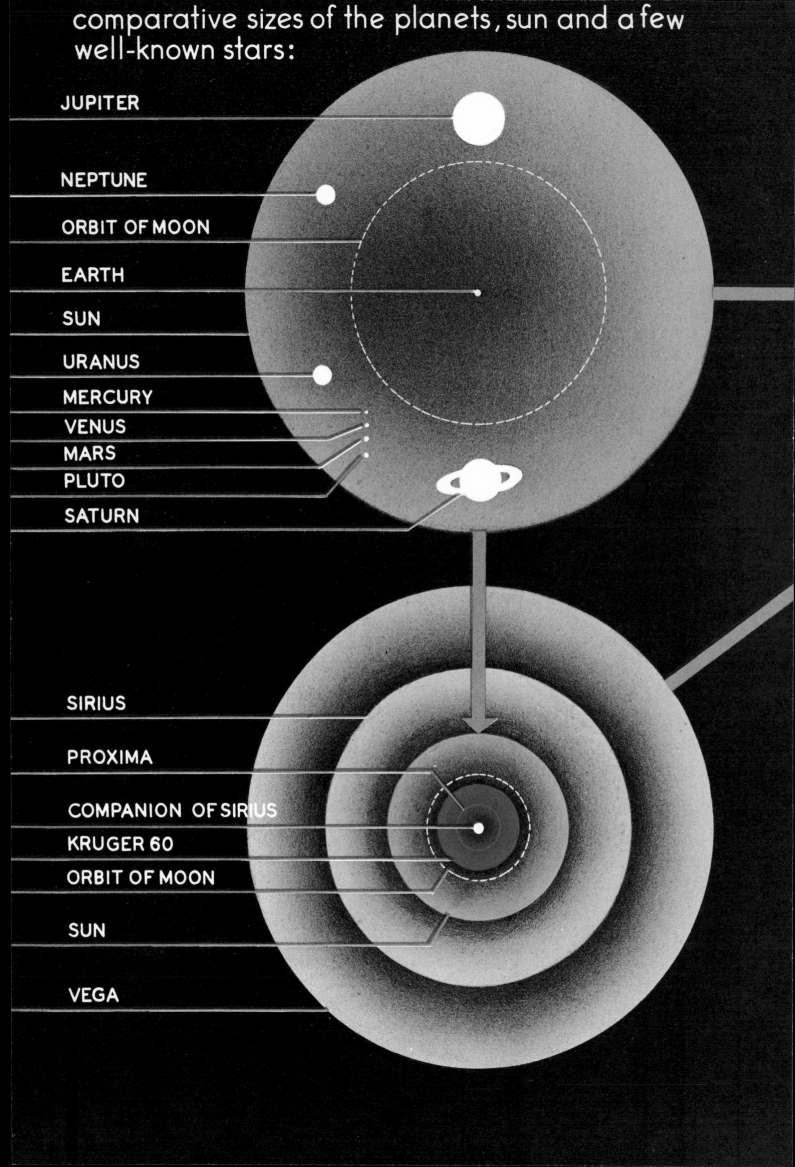

comparative sizes of the planets, sun and a few well-known stars:

JUPITER

NEPTUNE

ORBIT OF MOON

EARTH

SUN

URANUS

MERCURY

VENUS

MARS

PLUTO

SATURN

SIRIUS

PROXIMA

COMPANION OF SIRIUS

KRUGER 60

ORBIT OF MOON

SUN

VEGA

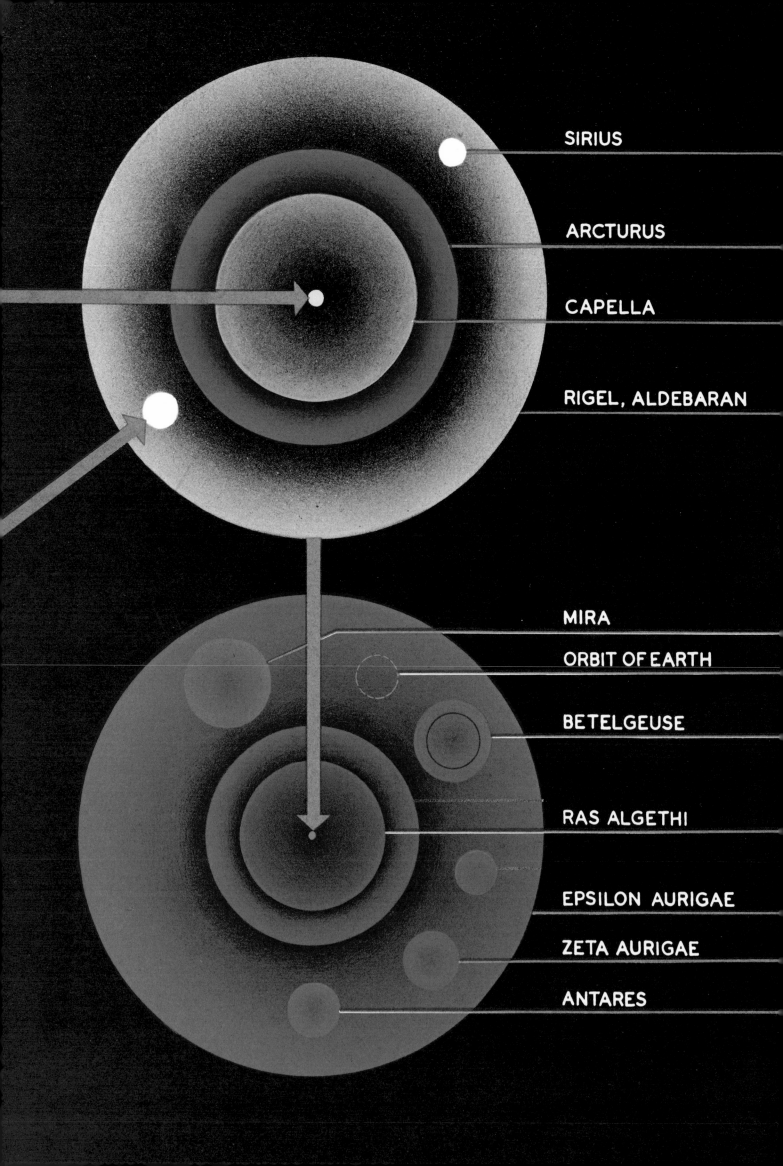

SIRIUS

ARCTURUS

CAPELLA

RIGEL, ALDEBARAN

MIRA

ORBIT OF EARTH

BETELGEUSE

RAS ALGETHI

EPSILON AURIGAE

ZETA AURIGAE

ANTARES

were being formed, and a time even earlier when there were no stars at all—perhaps some ten billion or more years ago. As the stars formed out of great clouds of gas and dust, so must the galaxy itself have formed out of a super-large gas and dust cloud. From what we now know, the globular clusters and the RR Lyrae stars were formed first, for they seem to be the oldest members of our galaxy, about ten billion years old. Stars like the Sun were formed some five billion years later.

As the galaxy had a beginning, it surely must some day come to an end. The first stars to fade into dimness as they go out are the energetic blue stars, which have short life-spans. Next, the yellowish stars like the Sun will begin to fade. At this stage, our galaxy will shine with a reddish light, for only the long-lived red stars will be left. But eventually they too must fade and go out. When that time comes, our galaxy will be a dim place, far too dim to be observed by astronomers of some other galaxy— if in that far distant time any astronomers remain in the universe.

Stars That Pulsate

As we found earlier, pulsating stars played the key role in the discovery of the distance to the center of our galaxy and the distance to the Andromeda Galaxy. Like giant, slow-beating hearts, these stars swell up and then shrink, becoming bright and then dim. They repeat this performance over and over again. The really large pulsating stars may take as long as two or three years to complete one cycle, or period, of swelling and shrinking. The smaller ones are quicker. They take only a few days, or even hours, to expand and contract. The fastest known pulsating star is SX Phoenicis. It has a period of only seventy-nine minutes. Although there are several different kinds of pulsating stars, we will mention only two kinds: the Cepheids and the RR Lyrae stars.

Considering that there are about 100 billion stars in our galaxy, pulsating stars seem to be rare. Only 10,000 or so have been discovered. And of the 10,000, about 500 are Cepheids. The stars were named "Cepheids" because the first star of this kind was discovered in the constellation Cepheus. The periods of Cepheids vary quite a bit. Some have periods slightly longer than twenty-four hours; the cycle of others is much longer, about fifty days. The period that seems to be most typical of these stars—at least those we observe in the flattened part of our galaxy—is about a week. All of the Cepheids pulsate so regularly, no matter what their period, that we could use them as an accurate clock.

A fascinating question, and one we cannot yet answer, is what makes pulsating stars pulsate? We now think that the Cepheids and other pulsating stars begin their adult lives in quite a normal way. Then at one stage they develop some kind of "chemical illness" and begin to throb. After perhaps millions of years the star recovers, stops pulsating, and begins to shine at a steady rate again.

The other major group of pulsating stars is made up of the RR Lyrae stars, which Shapley used as yardsticks to the globular clusters. We know of about 3000 RR Lyrae stars, more than a third of them belonging to the globular clusters. The rest are scattered throughout the galactic disc and belong to the crowded nucleus of the galaxy. The RR Lyrae variables have much shorter periods than the Cepheids. The shortest periods are about eight hours, the longest ones about sixteen.

Among the other types of variable stars are the Red Variables, which have very long periods. These stars are red giants and have periods that range between 100 and 1000 days. If you are an amateur astronomer you can do some very useful work by observing variable stars. The telescopes of big observatories are used for "more important" work; as a result, amateur astronomers have taken over the systematic observation of variable stars. Information about what they do can be obtained from the AAVSO (American Association of Variable Star Observers).

Double Stars

In size and brightness our Sun is a rather ordinary star that moves through the galaxy with a group of other stars. More than two-thirds of all the stars in our galaxy belong to partner systems, or are members of a family of stars staying rather closely together. Sometimes star families have hundreds of members. Yet many of the families do not exceed two, three, or four stars. Among the most interesting stars having companions are the double stars.

When two stars are situated close together and circle about each other they are called a *double star* or *binary* pair. Sometimes their close

45

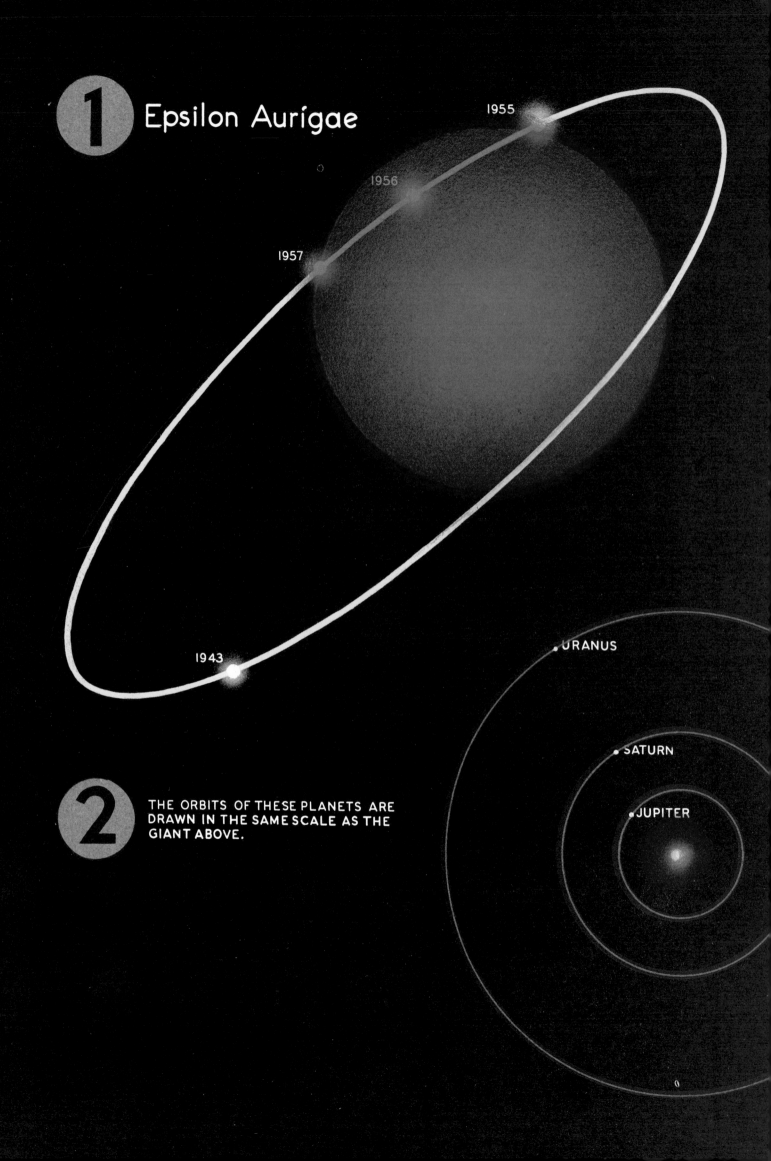

association causes them to shoot out long colorful streamers of gas. One of the most exciting displays of this type is the double star known as Beta Lyrae, made up of a large blue star and a smaller yellow one. The larger star ejects luminous gas which glows red against the blackness of space. The smaller one captures some of the gas, with the result that the two stars must be circled by a narrow red belt. The gas which the smaller star does not keep is probably hurled out in a mammoth red spiral. Beta Lyrae is only one of several double stars known to put on such a colorful show.

Any two stars that seem to be very close to one another are considered binary stars. However, there are some that only *appear* to be close together; actually they are not. Some night, find the star Mizar, which forms the bend in the handle of the Big Dipper. If you do not stare directly at Mizar but look a little bit away from it, you can just make it out to be two stars. Because of our line of sight, Mizar and the other star, Alcor, appear to be twins; actually they are many, many light-years away from each other. Such stars that appear double, but really are not, are called *optical* binaries. In the 1800s when astronomers began examining stars with spectroscopes, they took a close look at Mizar, ignoring Alcor, and discovered that Mizar itself was made up of two stars forming a true binary. The two stars forming Mizar were seen to be revolving around each other. Today we know that one of the stars is itself a true binary, so Mizar is made up of at least three stars.

As we saw earlier, another true binary system is made up of the blue star Sirius, known as the Dog Star, and a white-dwarf companion called the Pup. The smaller star is so dense that a tablespoon-sized chunk of it would weigh more than a ton on the Earth! The granddaddy of all the double stars is Epsilon Aurigae. One of its stars is a yellow supergiant 250 times bigger than our Sun. But its companion is even bigger—3000 times the size of the Sun. Many of the stars we see each night are actually double or triple stars, yet the naked eye sees them as a single star. The North Star, for example, is actually made up of three stars. Castor is made up of six.

47

Visitors from Outer Space

Meteoroids, Meteors, and Meteorites

Several tons of material from space fall onto the Earth each day. Most of it ends up as fine dust that drifts down through the atmosphere. Some of it, however, is material the size of sand grains and pebbles. Occasionally, chunks of rock and metal the size of houses or small mountains crash into our planet with explosive force. The largest outer space visitor on display is the Ahnighito Meteorite. It is a chunk of metal weighing thirty-four tons and is on permanent exhibit at The American Museum—Hayden Planetarium. An even larger one is in South Africa.

Where does all of this material come from? And what happens when a small space mountain plummets into us? For convenience, we can talk about "big stuff" and "little stuff." Let's take up the big stuff first.

Between the planets Mars and Jupiter is a belt of debris orbiting the Sun just as the planets do. How the debris (called the *asteroids*) got there, we do not know. Some astronomers have suggested that a planet once occupied the orbit between Mars and Jupiter and was broken up by Jupiter's gravitational attraction. Other astronomers suspect that the original matter occupying that particular region of the Solar System never collected itself into a planet body when the Solar System was formed. Whatever the reason, it is there. Telescopic photographs of the asteroid belt show chunks of matter from fifty miles to several hundred miles across, and we can safely say that there must be millions and millions more asteroids only a few miles, a few yards, or a few inches from edge to edge. To date, astronomers have worked out the orbits of more than 3000 asteroids.

Planets close to the asteroid belt—Jupiter, Mars, the Earth, and Moon—from time to time collide with asteroids. Mariner IV's remark-

48

This model shows the relative size of the asteroid Hermes and Manhattan Island, New York City.

The American Museum of Natural History

able photographs of Mars show that the planet's surface has several large craters. The Moon's surface is pockmarked with thousands upon thousands of craters. We now think that many of the craters on both Mars and the Moon were made by large asteroid impacts. The Earth, too, has many craters, but it has been only recently that we have begun to look for such impact craters on our home planet. One of the more spectacular and well preserved ones is the famous Barringer Crater near Winslow, Arizona. About 50,000 years ago an asteroid plunged into the Arizona desert with explosive impact and left the Barringer Crater scar: a gaping hole 600 feet deep and three-quarters of a mile from edge to edge.

To date we know of about fifty Earth craters in North America alone, thought to have been formed by stray asteroids. Some of them measure many miles from rim to rim, as the Moon's craters do. One scientist has even suggested that Hudson's Bay may be an old crater

49

carved out by an asteroid impact. Fortunately, these granddaddy collisions are rare events on the Earth nowadays. According to one estimate, we can expect one about every thousand years. But there may have been a time in the distant past when such collisions were more frequent.

The "little stuff," among which are the so-called "shooting stars," plunging into the Earth forms the bulk of the material reaching us from outer space. On just about any clear night, over a period of an hour, you can see anywhere from five to ten junior-sized visitors streak through the atmosphere. They are traveling so fast, up to 160,000 miles an hour, that most of them burn up before they reach the ground. They flare up at an altitude of about seventy-five miles, are visible for a second or so, and then disappear at a height of about fifty miles. Their fine remains drift to the ground as dust. The fleeting streak of light that a *meteoroid* leaves is called a *meteor*; and if the meteoroid survives its hot journey through the air and reaches ground, we call it a *meteorite*.

During many months of the year we have meteor showers. At such times it is possible to see dozens, and sometimes hundreds or thousands of meteors each hour. The Perseids Shower, which takes place around August 12 each year, is usually a good one, with fifty or more meteors streaking into view every hour. The Geminids Shower, which takes place around December 13, is also a good one. A meteor shower is named after the constellation out of which the meteors seem to flow. The Leonids Shower, for instance, which put on a remarkable display in November of 1966, is named after the constellation Leo. The swarm meteoroids, those producing meteor showers, are probably the remains of old comets and

The Barringer Crater, near Winslow, Arizona, was made by an asteroid that plunged into the desert with explosive impact about 50,000 years ago. It left a scar 600 feet deep.
The American Museum of Natural History

When the Andromeda Galaxy was being photographed at the Prague Observatory in 1923, an exceptionally bright meteor, called a "bolide," crossed the camera's field of view. The Prague Observatory

are about as soft as cigar ash. Whenever the Earth crosses the path of a swarm of these mushy meteoroids, we have a shower.

Comets

In May 1910, millions of people watched the return of Halley's Comet. What they saw was a bright point of light, about the size of a star, with a luminous tail stretching thousands of miles across the heavens. For many days Halley's Comet rose and set as the Sun does, then it disappeared from view. During Halley's time, and even during the 1910 return, many people were afraid of the comet, thinking that it was to bring world-wide disaster. Today we know that comets are among the most harmless objects in the sky.

The head, or *nucleus*, of a comet is nothing more than a loose swarm of stone and metal debris, each piece frosted over with frozen gas. Comets move in orbits about the Sun, but the orbits are usually long, stretched out ones. As a comet nears the Sun, the frost coatings are changed to a gas and the nucleus is seen to glow as it reflects light from the Sun. Some of the gas is pushed away from the nucleus by radiation pressure of the Sun and forms a long glowing tail. The gas tail is so thin that even faint stars can be seen through it. As the illustration of the orbit of Halley's Comet shows, the tail is always kept pointing away from the Sun. During each visit to the Sun the comet loses some of its gas; after a while so much is lost that we can no longer see the tail or head. In 1986 Halley's Comet is due to swing in close to the Sun again and should be visible to us. It will be interesting to see if we can notice a difference in the length of its tail.

Halley's Comet, as photographed on the night of May 15, 1910 in Honolulu.
Mount Wilson and Palomar Observatories

52

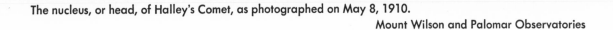

The nucleus, or head, of Halley's Comet, as photographed on May 8, 1910.

Mount Wilson and Palomar Observatories

One of the most unusual comets was Biela's Comet. It was first recorded in 1826 and is most likely the same comet that was seen in the years 1772 and 1805. As forecast by Biela, the comet came back six and three quarters years later, in 1832. But in 1839, when it was due for another return, it was difficult to see. However, in 1845 it was back again in full strength, although something had happened to it. It seemed to have split in two. While the smaller of the two heads became brighter, the larger one appeared to get dimmer. In addition, the two heads began drifting apart. By the time they made another return, in 1852, more than a million miles of space separated them. In 1859 and 1866, when the

53

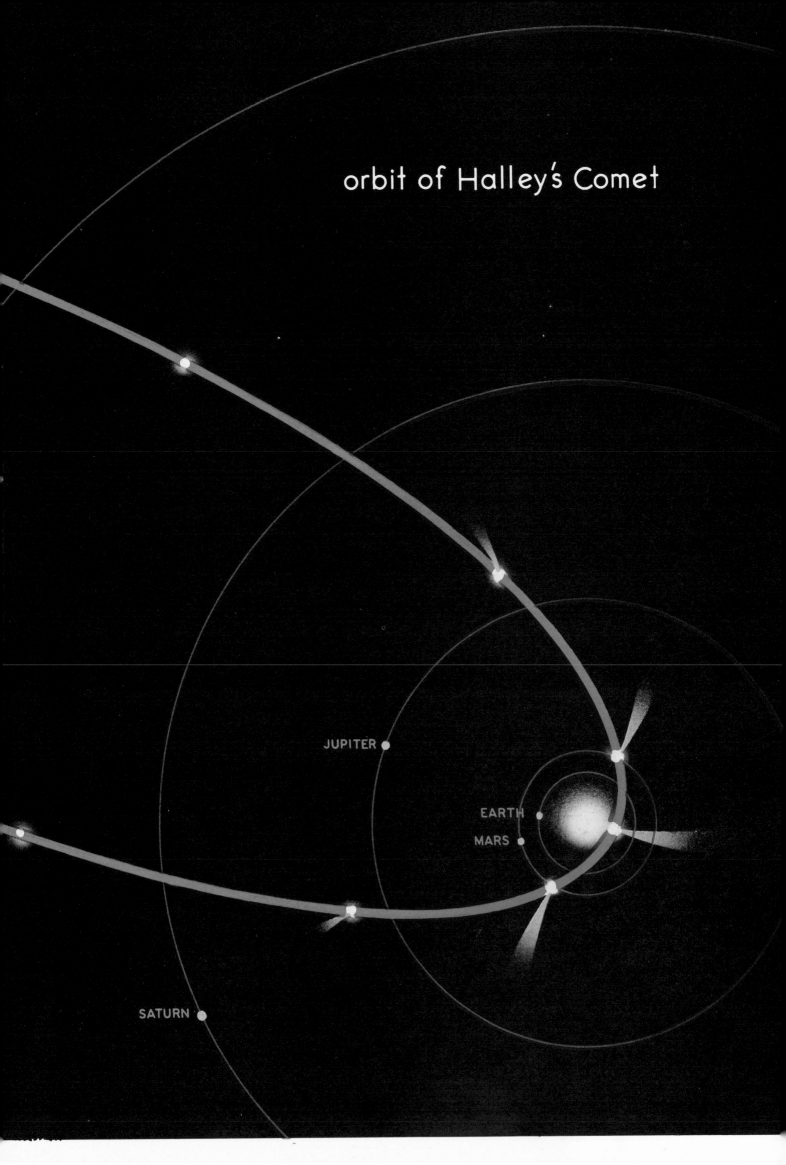

orbit of Halley's Comet

JUPITER

EARTH

MARS

SATURN

double comet was due back again, it did not appear either time. But in 1872, when it was also scheduled to make an appearance, there was a brilliant meteor shower!

So far in this book we have been concerned with many of the individual parts of the universe—comets, meteoroids, stars, nebulae, and galaxies. We have yet to ask about the universe as a whole. We find order and patterns within the Solar System and within galaxies. Do we also find order and a pattern to the billion or more galaxies that make up the bulk of the universe? How large is the universe? How was it formed? And what fate is in store for it?

"The Night the Sky Fell Down," a wood engraving of the meteor shower of the year 1883.

The American Museum of Natural History

The Runaway Universe

Distance to the Galaxies

There seems to be no end to the universe of galaxies. At least there seems to be no end to the number of galaxies we can see. Although only three galaxies are visible to the unaided eye, binoculars reveal several more. When the most powerful telescopes survey the sky, more than a billion galaxies can be seen. Telescopes even more powerful than the ones we now have would reveal a still greater number of galaxies.

Do we find order or patterns when we survey the universe of galaxies? The Sun, remember, belongs to a local group of stars. The stars forming our local group are moving every which way in relation to each other, but the group as a whole shares a common motion around the galaxy. As the individual bees in a swarm are moving every which way in relation to each other, the swarm itself moves as a whole. The same can be said of clusters of galaxies.

As there are globular clusters of stars, each cluster containing about 100,000 stars, there are also clusters of galaxies. In the constellation Virgo cluster is a neighbor, only 40 million light-years away. The Coma cluster is a bit farther away, some 220 million light-years. A cluster in Hydra is much farther away, more than a billion light-years. And the ular cluster of stars, the Coma cluster of galaxies is most crowded near the center and least crowded out toward the edge. In all, we know of more than 3000 clusters of galaxies! We find them all over the sky. The Virgo cluster is a neighbor, only forty million light-years away. The Coma cluster is a bit farther away, some 220 million light-years. A cluster in Hydra is much farther away, more than a billion light-years. And the most distant cluster we know of (3C 295) seems to be nearly six billion light-years away. At the present time, then, that is the observable size of the universe—a great sphere of galaxies that seems to spread out from us to a distance of about six billion light-years.

How Do the Galaxies Move?

By 1930 astronomers had studied enough galaxies to be sure about one thing. Although a few nearby galaxies are approaching us, all of the others are racing away at extremely high speeds. While the Sun's speed around the galaxy is about 600,000 miles an hour, many galaxies are racing away from our own at speeds of thirty-five *million* miles an hour. Astronomers discovered something else, as well. The farther away from us a galaxy, or cluster of galaxies is, the greater its speed away from us. Listed here are six galaxies and six clusters of galaxies. They are arranged in the order of distance from us. As the distance becomes greater, what happens to the speed of the galaxy or cluster? (The distances are given in *millions* of light-years, and the speeds are given in *miles per second*. The galaxy M64, for example, is seven million light-years away and has a speed of 93 miles a second.)

Galaxy	Speed	Distance	Cluster	Speed	Distance
M64	93	7	Perseus	3,370	179
M82	186	13	Pegasus II	7,900	490
M63	280	18	Corona Borealis	13,500	820
M65	500	25	Ursa Major 2	25,000	1,560
M96	590	29	Hydra	37,500	1,960
M60	680	38	3C 295	85,600	5,700

No matter in what part of the sky we point our telescopes, the picture is the same—galaxies and clusters of galaxies rushing away from us at tremendous speeds. To visualize what astronomers see, picture a half-inflated balloon with small paper dots stuck onto it, the dots representing the galaxies. As the balloon is inflated and expands, the distance between the dots becomes greater.

Imagine yourself on one of these galaxy-dots, any one. Every other galaxy-dot around you would appear to be moving away. From your position you would seem to be at the center of things, at the center of an expanding universe. And if you moved to another galaxy you would see exactly the same thing. No matter which galaxy you chose, the view would be the same. Every galaxy would appear to be at the center of a universe that is expanding at breakneck speed.

Let's stop and think about all of this for a moment. What does it

58

all mean? A very important law of physics tells us that the highest possible speed is the speed of light—186,000 miles a second. Nothing can move faster than that. Now look back to the list of galaxies and clusters again and read down the speed column. The highest speed we find is that for the cluster 3C 295. From what we can tell, it is moving at 85,600 miles a second, more than half the speed of light. What if there are galaxies even more distant than 3C 295? If there are, we would expect them to be moving away from us at an even greater speed. And if there are galaxies still farther away, they must be moving even faster. Carrying on in this way—if our thinking is correct—we would eventually be imagining galaxies moving at the speed of light, and faster! Here is one of the places where we begin to run into trouble.

Another trouble area is time. If we look at the Hydra cluster of galaxies tonight, we do not see that cluster as it is now. The light reaching us tonight from that distant cluster started out on its journey nearly two million years ago. And the light leaving that cluster tonight will not reach us for nearly two million years from now. So when we look at the very distant galaxies and clusters we are seeing them as they were long, long ago. We have no way of knowing what they are like now, or if they are still moving in the way their light reaching us tonight tells us that they were moving thousands and millions of years ago.

These are only two of the problems astronomers have to puzzle over when they try to understand what the universe is, what it was like in the distant past, and what it will be like in the distant future on a time scale we find difficult to understand.

Help from "Quasars"?

In the early 1960s astronomers discovered a new class of objects in the heavens—*quasars*. What they are we cannot yet say, but they may cause us to change some of our ideas about the universe.

According to what we know about them now, the quasars seem to be the most distant objects, and the brightest. Although smaller than any typical galaxy, the quasars appear to be up to 100 times brighter than the brightest galaxies we can see. If we work out their speeds and distances in the same way that we work out the speeds and distances of the other galaxies, the quasars appear to be rushing away from us at speeds greater than the speed of light. Something must be wrong, but what?

We now think that the methods we use to measure the speeds and distances of most of the galaxies and clusters break down when we try to use those methods to measure the distance and speed of objects in the farthest reaches of the universe.

Using a different set of rules, astronomers now guess that the quasars might be moving away from us at speeds of about 150,000 miles a second, but we don't know. If such speeds are correct, then the quasars would be about ten billion light-years away. Ten billion years ago, when the quasars were emitting the light reaching us tonight, our galaxy was just being formed. If all galaxies are about the same age, and if the quasars are galaxies, we may be looking back ten billion years in time and seeing a galaxy being formed. We may be witnessing an event that took place before we were born! Right now we simply do not know. It may turn out that quasars are not galaxies at all.

How Old Is the Universe?

At least twice in this book we have said that our home galaxy is about ten billion years old. We have also hinted that all of the galaxies might be about the same age. If we are right, then there must have been a time when there were no galaxies. What was the universe like then? Or to put the question another way, was there a universe at all?

Astronomers are in pretty good agreement about several things: 1. that stars are born out of the nebulae, shine for tens of millions or for billions of years, then die; 2. that galaxies, too, are born out of supernebulae, then after billions of years fade to dimness as their stars go out one by one; 3. that the universe of galaxies is expanding, and that we would see galaxies rushing away from us in all directions, no matter what galaxy happened to be our home; 4. that all of the galaxies we can see are distributed fairly evenly through space. There are as many in any one direction of the sky as there are in any other direction.

What all of this means is another matter. There isn't very much agreement about a pattern of time and a pattern of space for the universe. In a way, we are in a fix similar to the fix the old Greek astronomers were in, only ours is on a much larger scale. The Greeks could see the paths traced by the planets across a chalkboard-sky, a sky that appeared to have a surface; but they were not able to envision those paths in three-dimensional space. Today we can detect certain motions of the galaxies—a general rushing away from us and from each other—but we cannot envision a shape or limit to the space occupied by the galaxies.

A Steady-State Universe: What if the galaxies are not all the same age? What if the shapes—spherical, elliptical, spiral—are clues to their ages? Then some of the galaxies we now see are old, some young, and others in between. While some are dying and fading out of sight, others are being born. According to the steady-state theory, there is enough gas and dust between the galaxies to form new galaxies. As ten, twenty, or a thousand galaxies fade from view, ten, twenty, or a thousand new ones are being formed and filling the "gaps." In this way the number of galaxies in any given region of space remains pretty much the same. This theory pictures a universe which has always been pretty much as it is today and which will remain more or less the same forever.

If the steady-state picture is the right one, then there must be a lot of very old galaxies out there, glowing a dull red because their short-lived blue and yellow stars have spent themselves. So far, no one has seen such a dimming galaxy, but then no one had recognized the unusual nature of quasars until the 1960s. At this time we cannot say for certain that a steady-state universe is impossible.

A Big-Bang Universe: The most distant galaxies are seen to be rushing away from us the fastest; the nearer ones are moving away more slowly. Suppose, for a moment, that we can reverse time and make it run backward. The galaxies suddenly stop dead in their tracks, then they begin to back up, each one moving in toward us at exactly its rushing-away speed. If we imagine the galaxies to continue moving this way, what is bound to happen? They would retrace their paths and eventually come together in our region of space.

If we suppose that all of the galaxies actually were together in our region of space at some distant time in the past, when was it? When we examine the speeds and distances of a great many of the galaxies and clusters of galaxies, we find that nearly every one began its outward journey about ten billion years ago. If the Hydra cluster, for example, had set out from our region of space ten billion years ago, and if it has been traveling around 37,500 miles a second ever since, it would now be two billion light-years away. And that is the distance from us at which we find it now.

We can now return to our balloon model of an expanding universe,

OUR GALAXY

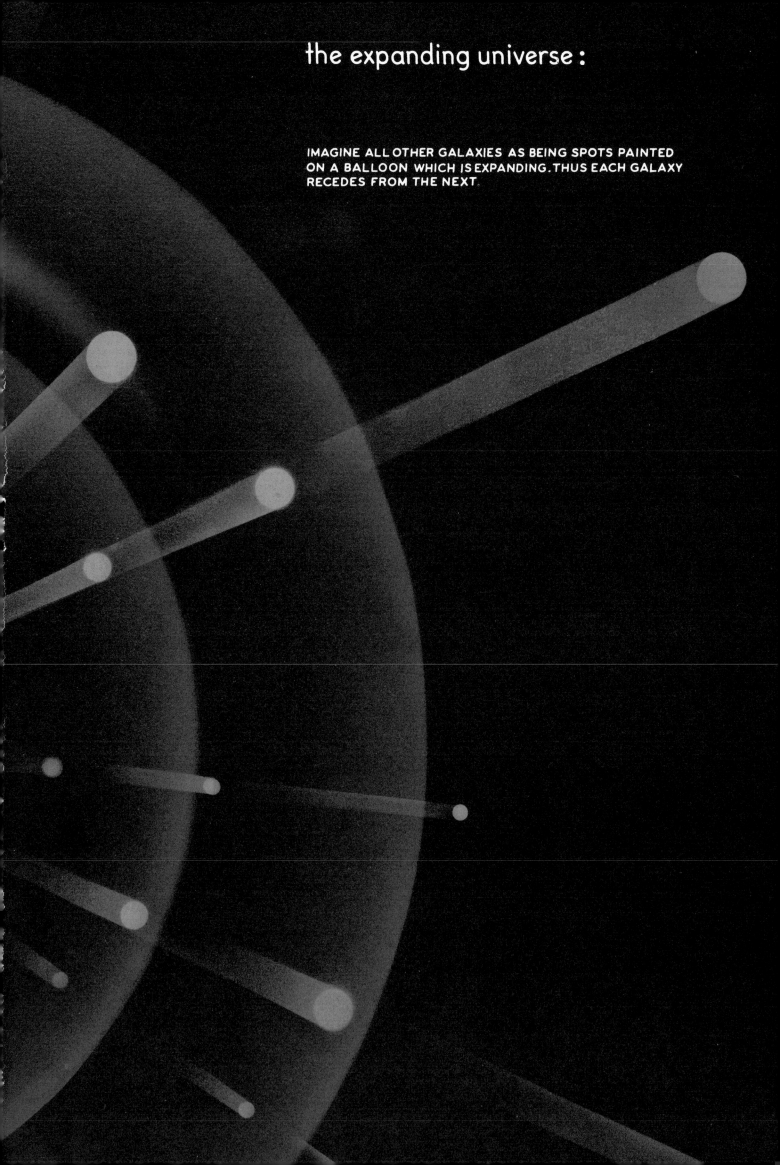

the expanding universe:

IMAGINE ALL OTHER GALAXIES AS BEING SPOTS PAINTED
ON A BALLOON WHICH IS EXPANDING. THUS EACH GALAXY
RECEDES FROM THE NEXT.

but now we want to make it a *shrinking* universe. As the balloon deflates and becomes smaller, each galaxy-dot moves closer to its neighbor. And so the process continues until all of the galaxy-dots are very close together and occupy a small sphere of space. According to the big-bang theory, this was the state of cosmic affairs about ten billion years ago. And just before that there were no galaxies, just a great super-dense cloud of gas. Something caused the cloud to expand violently and rush outward in all directions. Some of the gas formed clouds, which became the galaxies. Within each galaxy-cloud still smaller clouds gave birth to star clusters and to individual stars. And as some of the individual stars formed, "leftover" gas and dust packed itself into planets. Some of the gas and dust never formed stars, and remains as the nebulae to this day.

In our brief lifetime, a mere tick of the cosmic clock, we see ourselves as part of a universe that is expanding. But what happens next? Some astronomers say that the galaxies may keep on rushing outward in all directions, without end. In a long cosmic sigh the universe may be gradually dispersing, or spreading ever outward. Others have said that the expansion eventually will slow down and stop. The galaxies will then begin to move back toward the region where they were formed. They will all come together and be pressed into a mammoth elastic sphere which will explode, and the process will start all over again.

Like the steady-state theory, this version of the big-bang theory has us living in a universe without beginning or end. We are told that about ten billion years ago a big bang began a new cycle, and that tens of billions of years from now, when all of the galaxies tumble in toward the center again, another big bang will begin the cycle anew, on and on forever.

Which view is correct, we cannot say. Perhaps neither, perhaps a bit of each. In their exploration of the universe, the astronomer and the physicist are at two great frontiers of science today. Having pulled the atom to bits and pieces, the physicist is now trying to discover a pattern. But the more he looks, the more bits and pieces he finds and the more confusing the picture seems to become. At the opposite end of the scale, the astronomer also is trying to fit bits and pieces together to find a pattern, but the more he finds, the more confusing the picture becomes for him also. Each, in his way, is exploring worlds that could not be imagined before the beginning of this century. By the end of it perhaps we will understand a little more than we do now.

Index

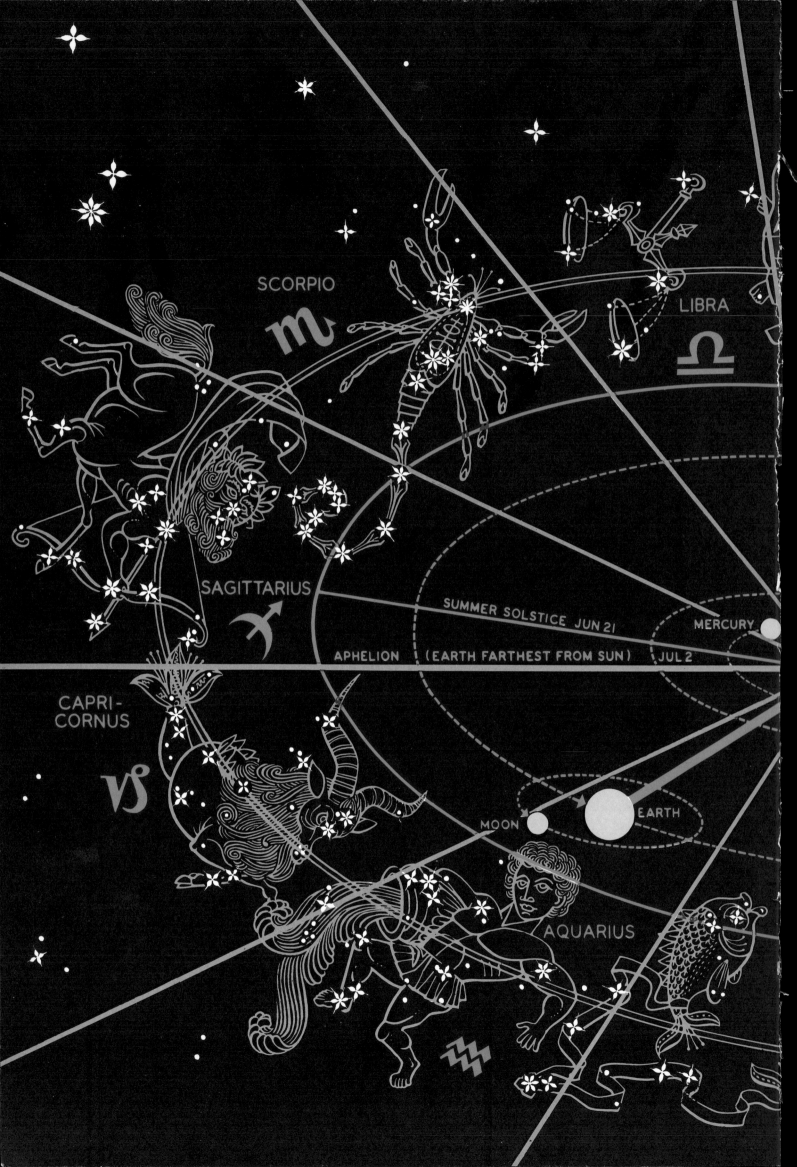

SCORPIO

♏

LIBRA

♎

SAGITTARIUS

♐

SUMMER SOLSTICE JUN 21

MERCURY

APHELION   (EARTH FARTHEST FROM SUN)   JUL 2

CAPRI-
CORNUS

♑

MOON   EARTH

AQUARIUS

♒